# Midnight Marquee #75

# MIDNIGHT MARQUEE
## Number 75

**Editors**
Gary J. Svehla
Susan Svehla

**Managing Editor**
Richard J. Svehla

**Copy Editor**
Linda J. Walter

**Graphic Design Interior**
Gary J. Svehla

**Cover Design/ Title Page Design**
Susan Svehla

**Contributing Writers**
Anthony Ambrogio, Mark Clark, Bruce Dettman, Arthur Joseph Lundquist, Greg Mank, Gary D. Rhodes, Brian Smith, Gary J. Svehla, Steven Thornton

**Acknowledgments**
John Antosiewicz Photo Archives, Eric Caidin, Jerry Ohlinger's Movie Material Store, Greg Mank, Photofest/Buddy Weiss

**Illustrator**
Allen J. Koszowski

**Publisher**
Midnight Marquee Press

*Midnight Marquee*
Number 75
Copyright 2006 © by Gary J. Svehla

Published twice yearly by Midnight Marquee Press at $17 per year. Printed by Thomson-Shore, Dexter, Michigan.

Return postage must accompany articles and art, if the owner wants them returned. No responsibility is taken for unsolicited material. Editorial views expressed by our contributors are not necessarily those of the publisher. Nothing may be reproduced in any media without written permission of the publisher. Send submissions of articles, letters and art to Gary J. Svehla, 9721 Britinay Lane, Baltimore, MD 21234; web site: http://www.midmar.com; e-mail: mmarquee@aol.com

Letters of comment addressed to Midnight Marquee or Gary or Susan Svehla will be considered for publication unless the writer requests otherwise. Subscription rates: $10 per single copy or $17 per year (shipped U.S. Media Mail). Subscription copies are mailed in sturdy cardboard mailers and will arrive in excellent condition; support MidMar by becoming a direct-mail subscriber. Foreign orders are $39 (U.S.) for a two-issue subscription. This issue is dedicated to fantastic artist and friend Allen J. Koszowski, who is on the mend.

## TABLE OF CONTENTS

**3** Marquee Mutterings: Editorial
by Gary J. Svehla

**5** Groundbreakers: The 13 Most Influential Horror Movies
by Gary J. Svehla

**16** Lugosi vs. Karloff—Eternally!
by Gary D. Rhodes

**23** Forum/Against 'Em—*The Wolf Man*
edited by Anthony Ambrogio

**40** Evelyn Moriarty Remembers Carl Laemmle, Jr.—Universal's Crown Prince
by Gregory Mank

**47** The Three Faces of Universal's Dracula
by Brian Smith

**57** DVD Reviews
by Gary J. Svehla

Retro becomes techno!

A few years ago, while meeting people at conventions, exchanging emails and speaking to peers on classic film related message boards, every movie collector expressed views on whether they trade in their VHS collection for DVDs (now a moot point of course). In 2006 the hot discussion is should I trade in my DVDs for HD-DVD or Blu-Ray high definition ones?

During this past summer I had an intense conversation with one of our regular customers over the phone, and he argued he has put too much money into his VHS collection, and damn if he will convert to DVD. In all seriousness he said that he didn't like the look of DVDs and that VHS quality was plenty fine for him. Perhaps if you are watching movies on an iPod or 13-inch analog TV screen! But this fellow was watching VHS tapes on a 60-inch LCD monitor! Besides the lower resolution smeary presentation, VHS tapes are more than obsolete simply because their presentation is generally substandard. Movies on VHS are rarely presented in their original aspect ratio and surround sound, and even digital audio cleanup is rare if impossible. Watch an Argento or Bava movie on VHS and see a truncated, bastardized version compared to the uncut, European edition with the original soundtrack restored on DVD, with the added option of selecting a dubbed or subtitled version. And remember when VHS tapes cost $100 for such sliced-and-diced editions as compared to $20 for a special edition DVD?!!!!!

So why replace DVDs when they are digitally close to perfection in both audio and visual presentation? DVDs feature the original aspect ratio presentation, are uncut and mostly unrated. So why even think of once again replacing our collection?

Surprisingly, most collectors feel replacing and upgrading is silly, a corporate blood-sucking ploy where technology makes everything obsolete every decade, if not sooner. Replacing a movie collection is very expensive and not everyone can afford to do this. And now with the 1080p high definition revolution with HD-DVD warring against Blu-Ray for consumer dollars, why should we even consider replacing our recently purchased 75th Anniversary editions of *Frankenstein* and *Dracula* with high definition versions most likely to be offered within the coming 12 months. Come on, most say, high definition might be preferable for new films such as *V For Vendetta, Sin City, Shaun of the Dead* and *The Sixth Sense*. But not for the Val Lewton B classics and the entire spectrum of Universal and Hammer classics, right? Such vintage horror and science fiction movies would look good enough in standard definition 480p, right?

Buddy, think again!

In the past month I switched from DirecTV (with whom I have been a customer for 12 years) to the Dish Network, citing the availability of over twice as much HD programming, most notably the Voom HD network including the Monsters HD channel (which shows movies, too many modern ones unfortunately, remastered in 1080i high definition). The critical question here is whether Universal horror classics of the 1930s and 1940s look that much better in HD compared to standard definition DVDs.

I put the two to the test, and here is what my *naked* eye discerned.

Last weekend Monsters HD ran an entire weekend of Universal horror classics including the 1940s *Mummy* series, *The Wolf Man, Frankenstein Meets the Wolf Man*, etc. What I did was get my Universal Legacy box sets and set my DVDs to coincide with the HD screenings of the same Universal classic. With a click of my remote I could toggle between component 1 (my DVD player) and component 2 (my Dish Network connection)... I temporarily disconnected my regular Dish Network HDMI connection to be fair. So I was able to toggle between the Wolf Man sequences showing Larry caught in the trap and being rescued by the Gypsy Woman and later pursuing the lovely Evelyn Ankers through the foggy woods. And here is what I found.

The Monsters HD presentations were visibly superior (even to my wife Sue's eyes, and she's not into the subtlety of technology as I am) in every instance, every sequence and every movie scanned.

Superior, how?

The Monsters HD presentation was crisper and sharper... not only in the focused foreground but also in the middle areas and background, where the photography is always slightly softer. In the HD presentation the sharpness layers are uniformly richer, almost creating a 3-D effect so now the audience's eye could scan foreground, mid-ground and background with equal clarity (of course what was photographed as being slightly out of focus is still softly rendered, but far less so). But the superiority did not only appear in areas of sharpness and clarity (seeing facial pores and subtly of makeup execution is amazing). The contrast between blacks (deep, rich blacks) and whites were equally superior with the HD presentation. What

sentations. Darn, even lower-budgeted AIP chestnuts such as *Blood of Dracula* are startling in HD, presented in the original widescreen 185:1 aspect ratio, with depth and sharpness that is almost surreal. HD, if done right, even makes schlock look terrific.

I cannot speak for others (budget is a prime consideration here), but when the opportunity arises for me to purchase HD versions of all the classic, and not so classic, horror and science fiction movies from the Golden Age, I will be first in line to upgrade, because HD is superior. Don't take my word for it… watch the Monsters HD channel on Dish Network and see for yourself. I guarantee you won't look back!

appeared to be grayed out or slightly overexposed or too muddy become clearly defined with the HD presentation and once again the difference between video presentation and a 35mm film became less distinct. Perhaps even more than sharpness, the better-defined contrast detail becomes the prime factor in the superiority of the HD source. The major flaw between 35mm film and home video is the inability of video to produce true blacks, but this flaw is becoming less and less distinct. The HD source produced a more film-like grain that once again created the illusion of 35mm film stock. And remember, I watch my movies projected on a large nine-foot-wide screen.

Imagine the shock of the first time viewing a remastered version of *Frankenstein* or even *Ghost of Frankenstein* on DVD and thinking, my God, this is akin to seeing the movie for the very first time. Now the upgrade to HD is not as startling as the upgrade from VHS to DVD, but the upgrade is startling nonetheless. And as I said, even to the untrained novice's eye, the HD improvement is very noticeable.

So everyone out there who thinks that HD only benefits modern movies, think again. I am afraid that even the Monogram Lugosi Nine will look terrific in HD pre-

And may I offer my humble apologies for the lateness of this issue. With only Sue and me manning the offices and producing several new titles in our book line, and with the production of *Terror in the Pharaoh's Tomb* consuming most of our time, the magazines had to be pushed back. Never fear, *Midnight Marquee* may be delayed, but it will always be forthcoming. Thank you for your patience, and I hope to return to a more normal production schedule during the next 12 months.

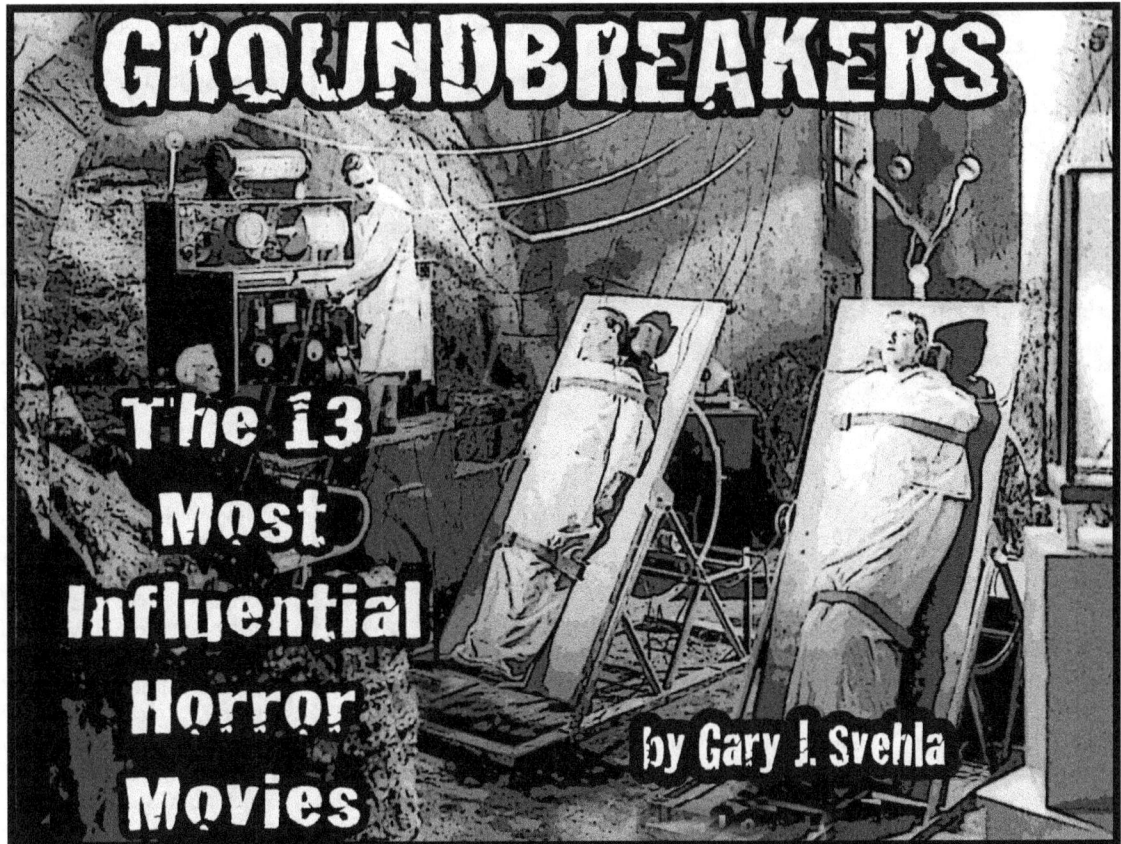

# GROUNDBREAKERS
## The 13 Most Influential Horror Movies
### by Gary J. Svehla

My wife Susan wanted me to give a "guest" talk at the 2005 FANEX classic horror film convention in Baltimore, and I wanted to speak about an article idea I had brewing. I needed to bounce these ideas around and receive audience feedback. In my mind I was mulling over the 13 most influential horror movies of all time, movies I soon began to refer to as groundbreakers. No, I was not speaking about my favorite films or even the very best ones. My thesis would concern those groundbreaking horror movies that pushed the genre ahead creatively into new vistas of artistic expression. Those movies that ignited sub-genres or created a new type of horror movie that was not one of a kind but became a mover and shaker that inspired a slew of many others. And to make this a challenge for me, I decided that I was only allowed 13 movies that covered the horror film genre from 1930 until 2000... a mere baker's dozen. So, here in chronological order, are, in my estimation, the 13 groundbreaking horror movies of all time. As always, feedback is appreciated.

*Dracula*, released on Valentine's Day 1931, started the Universal Pictures horror film cycle, so why do I select *Frankenstein*, released later the same year, as the first groundbreaking horror film? My difficult decision was deciding which one of the two would be selected, but *Frankenstein* became my choice. First of all, even though *Dracula* is a horror film classic, it wasn't meant to be and it certainly wasn't sold as one. Remember, Bela Lugosi was marketed as the romantic mystery man, the Valentino of the Dead and *Dracula* was released on Valentine's Day. While the first 20 minutes of the film and final five are grounded with horror film imagery (those ghoulish lines of dialogue, the dusty old castle with its haunted staircase, and the Count's eager anticipation when Renfield cuts his finger and blood appears), the remainder of the movie is played more darkly romantic, with Lugosi's Dracula depicted as a cruel Old World European Count.

*Frankenstein*, in contrast, is played as pure horror mythos. The film features the obsessive mad scientist who dares to dabble in God's domain, and while we had the evil Acolyte Renfield in *Dracula*, the Renfield character starts out perfectly normal until he goes insane and develops an urge to consume little lives. Dwight Frye's Fritz in *Frankenstein* is twisted and demented from the get-go, a sadist who loves to inflict pain upon the pathetic revived-from-the-dead corpse. And while Dracula could double as a romantic mystery figure, Boris Karloff's monster is purely undead, a reanimated corpse becoming a child reborn trying to learn how to live again. We have the Gothic watchtower, the evil scientific laboratory with brains floating in jars, teachers and fiancées who try to cure the obsessive whims of Dr. Frankenstein, graveyards and decaying gallows victims. All the components of the burgeoning horror film genre appear in *Frankenstein*. *Dracula*, on the other hand, disguises and even sublimates its horror film roots. Yes, Dracula is undead, a vampire, but he is portrayed as a powerful East European gentleman, albeit a savage one.

**Colin Clive, Edward Van Sloan and Boris Karloff from *Frankenstein***

But he's not necessarily a monster, a horror figure; at least the Universal production does not play up those aspects. My point is a simple one. Had *Dracula* remained the hit it was without a *Frankenstein* (or other distinct horror movies) to follow it up, *Dracula* alone would not have inspired the Universal horror factory to invent the classic horror film genre. True, *Dracula* came first, but the picture played its horror genre cards too lightly, too politely, always trying to be a morbidly romantic film first and a horror film second. *Frankenstein* was always marketed as a horror film and its romantic elements are secondary to the evil compulsions of the Byronic hero who pushes his true love into the arms of bland romantic lead John Boles. *Dracula* opened the door for Bela Lugosi to portray other corruptible, powerful romantic leads. *Frankenstein* opened the door for Boris Karloff to play other monsters. And finally, the direction by master James Whale created more of an idiosyncratic production where Whale was free to instill more blatant horror elements into his production without having to disguise them. *Frankenstein*, more so than *Dracula*, created the overall Universal horror look and introduced the iconic horror characters.

Our second groundbreaking horror movie, *The Black Cat* (1934), also a Universal Picture, forwards the concept of the horror film star (in this case Bela Lugosi and Boris Karloff) and the concept of the stylized eccentricity of future horror films (eccentric in both visual look and theme). First, with Universal in the 1930s and 1940s and Hammer in the 1950s and 1960s, the concept of actors primarily known for their performances in horror cinema came to light with *The Black Cat*. Performers such as Karloff, Lugosi, John Carradine, Lionel Atwill, George Zucco and later Vincent Price, Peter Cushing, and Christopher Lee, although they appeared in all sorts of movies, are principally renowned and remembered for their participation in horror movies, whose fans keep their memories alive. Lon Chaney was chiefly known as the Man of 1,000 Faces and remembered for his twisted, contorted and heavily made up performances. Even though he did play the Hunchback and the Phantom of the Opera, Chaney is not primarily known as a horror film icon. His work transcended the genre. However, Karloff and Lugosi are basically remembered for their horror movie performances, and the Universal publicity machine was aware of this

**Karloff as the emerging horror star in *The Black Cat***

fact and indeed marketed *The Black Cat* as the first teaming of the titans of terror. The publicity that showed both actors dressed as their horrific characters, playing a demonic game of chess and spitting out lines of dialogue that cleverly winked at their screen personas, only emphasized the fact that Lugosi and Karloff were the bricks and mortar of the Universal horror factory. Even though Karloff as Poelzig is portrayed as the Satan-worshipping fiend and Lugosi is seen as the more heroic Wertegast, it is Wertegast who binds and skins his adversary alive at the film's end in shadowy silhouette. Ultimately both actors are monstrous, horrifying and obsessed by their madness.

While *Dracula* was sanitized and safe and *Frankenstein* was iconic but not too morbid or cutting edge, Edgar Ulmer's *The Black Cat* created the concept of the eccentric, morbidly perverse theme for the horror genre. Look at the basic plot. We have Satanists in modern dress coming to watch the sacrifice of a young, beautiful girl. We have anecdotal war stories remembered of atrocities and horrible bloodshed. We have beautifully preserved corpses housed in glass cases in the cellar, the idea of necromancy implied. We have the villain killing the wife of his friend and then marrying his daughter… and then murdering his wife before her father can save her. While many of these perverse themes are subtly hinted at and merely discussed, their implications are clearly situated. As stated, the sequence where Lugosi skins the still-living Karloff in well-defined shadows, Karloff tied to a wooden rack as Lugosi's knife swishes up and down and sideways across Karloff's body as he gleefully rants and raves, becomes the earliest mainstream template for splatter cinema. *The Black Cat* is never polite and safe. It is a highly stylized visual exercise in horror, fueled by two incendiary performances of power and imagination. For me *The Black Cat* established the concept of horror film celebrity and forwarded the sense of gruesome unspeakable horrors of which *Frankenstein* could only hint.

**Wertegast (Bela Lugosi) skins Poelzig (Boris Karloff) alive in *The Black Cat*.**

Our third groundbreaking film is *King Kong* (1933), the RKO classic monster movie that heralded cinematic special effects (in this case the expert stop-motion animation created by master Willis O'Brien) as both the means and ends of monster cinema. *King Kong* directly inspired the sequel *Son of Kong* and the next decade's *Mighty Joe Young*, but more importantly, O'Brien influenced Ray Harryhausen to spearhead the giant monster invasion movies of the 1950s and beyond (*It Came from Beneath the Sea, The Beast from 20,000 Fathoms, 20 Million Miles to Earth*). And even more important than those giant stop-motion beasties of the 1950s, the special effects revolution instigated by the success of *Star Wars* in 1977 came as a direct result of *King Kong*, whose main character was a miniature model animated to interact with a cast of humans using seamless blue screen photography to marry the real and the animated. True, *The Lost World* came first, but *King Kong* also forwarded one of horror cinema's greatest themes—beauty and the beast, and the sensual and half-dressed Fay Wray became cinema's first damsel-in-distress scream queen, a woman whose performance is best known by her piercing scream. But most importantly, *King Kong* brought the most essential element to the special effects arena—personality and emotion, the human element. Missing from 1925's *The Lost World*, and missing from today's CGI effects before Peter Jackson, the animated King Kong becomes a truly living, breathing screen characterization, one that inspires audience sympathy. *King Kong* must be considered the third entry in our groundbreaker series simply for being the leader in special effects in the horror film cinema.

Our final Universal contribution to our list and fourth groundbreaker surfaces almost one decade later with *Frankenstein Meets the Wolf Man* (1943), the first of the studio's Monster Rally pictures. The theory here was a simple one. After running the gamut of creating new classic monsters (Count Dracula, Frankenstein's Monster, the Invisible Man, the Mummy, The Wolf Man), the marketing strategy was to combine several classic monster icons into one

The eighth wonder of the world...*King Kong*

movie. Such rally pictures would compensate for the lack of original ideas with the slam-bam approach of throwing several monsters into the mix. This represented Universal turning away from its adult-oriented artistic triumphs, those movies orchestrated by talented visionaries such as James Whale and Edgar Ulmer, and instead accepting the fact that they were a monster movie factory churning out a commodity. The B+ and B Universal romps of the 1940s constituted a marketing trend that would appeal to the younger audiences who did not wish to think too deeply and did not want to be frightened into submission (no human skinning here). These B formula monster rallies featured simplified stories, plenty of action and mood and a too rapidly concluded climax that finished off the monsters with floods, fires or explosions (not too easily resurrected logically, but monster rallies did not sweat such problems). *Frankenstein Meets the Wolf Man* was the absolute best of such rally pictures, featuring a compacted and high-interest plot with plenty of monster sequences featuring both the Wolf Man and Frankenstein's Monster. Universal had truly become a monster factory more focused on product than art and more concerned in turning out multiple movies instead of heralding one or two. Directors were now competent but never inspired and their job was to create as many hour- plus features as quickly as possible. For the remainder of the decade, culminating with *Abbott and Costello Meet Frankenstein*, the Universal monster rally was the name of the game since attempts to create classic monster franchises tanked with the Ape Woman series and the Rondo Hatton Creeper character. Even when Universal was not making monster rally entries (*Son of Dracula, She Wolf of London*), the monster factory B formula created by *Frankenstein Meets the Wolf Man* became the creative linchpin for the remainder of the decade.

With Universal relinquishing the adult horror film reins, rival studio RKO created a low-budget horror film unit presided over by producer/writer Val Lewton, with the goal of once again producing adult-themed horror entries, all on a budget. The first of these classic Lewton productions was *Cat People* (1942), a movie that established the formula for the other eight horror movie entries to be produced during the next five years. Some may argue that *Cat People* is a direct result of the success of Universal's *The Wolf Man*, and they would be correct. However, *The Wolf Man* was far from being a trendsetter; instead, it was the latest attempt to create a franchise monster that could restore Universal to the creative heights of *Frankenstein, The Mummy* and *The Invisible Man*. *The Wolf Man* arrived in the after-flow of the creative wave that produced those far superior horror entries, but Lewton's *Cat People* had very little to do with the look, theme or style of the inferior Universal entry.

*Cat People*, directed by Jacques Tourneur and scripted by DeWitt Bodeen, was anti-Universal in every aspect and becomes our fifth groundbreaker. For once, the concept of

**Bela Lugosi and Lon Chaney, Jr. in *Frankenstein Meets the Wolf Man*... the birth of the Monster Rally.**

monster did not exist or at least was ambiguous. The focus was on the horror within the psyche of the main characters, in this case a Serbian woman who believes sexual arousal will instigate the curse of her village, transforming her into a murderous panther. While the audience only briefly glimpses the animal in one sequence, the psychological turmoil suffered by Simone Simon's character Irena creates the overall sense of horror. After she marries good-guy Oliver, she is afraid to give in to her sexual longings and this prevents the consummation of her marriage. When Oliver has an affair with a female co-worker, Irena's passions are aroused and we have the terrifying silent walk where Alice is followed by something stalking her through the park until an intruding bus alleviates the tension. Later, Alice takes a swim in the cellar of her apartment building and is terrified by the animal-like shadows and slightly muted growling sounds. In Val Lewton's world, monsters and make-up are downplayed and psychological horrors reign supreme. Lewton's horror of suggestion focuses upon moody photography and editing that leads the viewing audience to think it sees and hears something that is ultimately vague and ambiguous. One thing that is not vague in Lewton's cinematic universe is the horror and chills created by such a style. Lewton's movies are filled with sequences influenced by ones in *Cat People* where Alice jumps out of her swimming pool, thinking her over-active imagination caused her fear, only to find her bathrobe ripped to shreds by some animalistic presence. Alice escapes the horror of her stalker in the park only to be scared out of her wits by the sudden sounds of bus brakes. Jacques Tourneur and Lewton always have the audience looking right when something suddenly comes to terrify us from the left. Lewton's monsters are always in human form and his horrors occur not in some mythological fairy tale country but in modern-day America, mostly the city. But once again, during the decade of the 1940s, the adult-oriented horror film returned to creative brilliance because of the Val Lewton horror factory.

Venturing into the 1950s, *The Thing* is one of the most important groundbreakers, our sixth, merging the horror and science fiction film genres. The vegetable alien, played by James Arness, combined the hulking brute strength of Frankenstein's Monster with the vampiric leanings of Count Dracula. The alien drains its human victims of blood that he feeds to his vegetative offspring in the greenhouse, so these creatures literally survive on human blood. Even though the creature is vastly intelligent, it does not desire to communicate with its human food, and Robert Cornthwaite's professor collapses like a rag doll when the creature smashes him with its arm. The direction by Christian Nyby (and the uncredited but very apparent Howard Hawks) sizzles with tension and apprehension, and the film is best remembered for its ensemble crew of actors and its overlapping dialogue that smacks of the Howard Hawks touch. *The Thing* features many classic sequences. The alien breaks free of its ice coffin when warm blankets are used to cover the monster's face that peers through the ice. We later have the startling shock of finding the ferocious fiend standing in wait by the greenhouse door when the military boys open it. The alien is set on fire and runs screaming through a window into the icy Arctic to safety. And eventually the conclusion involves a spectacular death sequence where the thing is electrified and burned to a cinder. What makes this movie groundbreaking is its single-minded depiction of alien visitors as vampiric breeders looking for a warm, cozy world to make their own. The vision of the alien visitor in *The Thing* is one of savagery, conquest, breeding and invasion. Instead of benevolent intelligent humanoid alien visitors, we have a Frankenstein Monster from space whose thoughts focus on genocide. Also, the concept of the claustrophobic horror movie was here defined as all the humans are trapped in this military camp in the frozen Arctic wasteland. Escape is impossible; the only hope for humankind is destroying the invader before its veggie-babies mature and multiply. At stake is nothing less than the survival of the human race, who must continue to "watch the skies" in preparation for future invasions. The military-based genre movie was born here, with films such as James Cameron's *Aliens* to follow in its wake. Indeed, even 1953's *Invaders from Mars* develops the military focus, and many of the giant-bugged monster films released by Hollywood during the decade featured

**James Arness as *The Thing***

military heroes. *The Thing* influenced so many other movies that followed.

During the 1950s horror movies were reinvented and targeted for youth and drive-in theater audiences, and while Roger Corman is one of the originators in this department, American-International must get the credit for advancing the low-budget exploitation movie in America during the decade of the 1950s. The movie I selected that characterizes the best aspects of that trend is *I Was A Teenage Werewolf*, produced by Herman Cohen and directed by Gene Fowler, Jr., our seventh groundbreaker. Why *I Was A Teenage Werewolf* and not a slew of other teenaged-based movies? To be honest, I could have easily justified *Earth vs. The Spider* or *Blood of Dracula*. But *I Was A Teenage Werewolf* specifically reinvents a classic Universal movie monster (the Wolf Man) for a new generation. The lead character of Tony Rivers (in a wonderful Michael Landon performance) reverberates with anger and angst of the same sort James Dean popularized in *Rebel Without a Cause*, and the screenplay focuses on the world of high school and teenagers. While adults play important parts (the father, the doctor, the police), the focus is always on the world and lives of teenagers and the film shows their point of view. The horror, as was now true, is scientifically motivated and not mythologically fabricated. No foggy Universal hamlets to be found here. The major horror sequence occurs in the high school gym, where a nicely curved gymnast hangs upside down from the parallel bars and watches in horror as Tony transforms into the drooling beast, one that is motivated more by his raging hormones than by any savage internal instincts. These exploitative movies always had some type of party or dance sequence with some lame performer singing the worst example of 1950s rock'n'roll. The adults are the evil ones, using teenagers as their experiments without compassion or personal concern. So the poor teenage experiment becomes both monstrous and sympathetic. And for once a rising young generation feels movies in Hollywood were being made specifically for them, and *I Was A Teenage Werewolf* shows just how the entire horror film genre was being turned on its ear and reinvented.

Hammer horror began with its black and white science fiction monster movies, primarily the Quatermass movies and *X, The Unknown* (and even earlier, *Four Sided Triangle* and *Spaceways*). But it wasn't until Hammer's second attempt to re-

**Michael Landon from *I Was a Teenage Werewolf***

visit Gothic traditional horror of the Universal variety that the company created our eighth groundbreaking film—*Horror of Dracula* (*Dracula* in the U.K.). The earlier *Curse of Frankenstein* used the same basic stars and production crew, but the results were less audacious and resonating. *Horror of Dracula* became a groundbreaking horror movie principally by creating an emotionally charged mythos of the undead. Never were vampires on the screen shown to be so intuitively undead and evil. The sequence where sizzling, nightgown-clad Valerie Gaunt, with her come-hither expressions and heaving bosoms, seemingly surrendering to the charms of the in-control Jonathan Harker (John Van Eyssen), is fairy tale damsel-in-distress dramatics. However, in a few moments, what Harker does not see, we, the audience see, and this fairy tale imagery suddenly becomes horrific. Gaunt's eyes lust lingeringly for the tender and exposed neck of Harker, as her romantic bedroom eyes suddenly become wide open with now a sly predatory aggression. Within a scant moment the sensual and defenseless victim has become the monstrous bloodsucker. As she bares her animalistic fangs and plunges for her unsuspecting victim's jugular, the former gentlemanly Count Dracula (Christopher Lee) now appears in full majestic glory, his lips and teeth smeared with blood, as he hisses with a look of animalistic intensity etched on his face of hatred and anger. This is a classic re-evaluation of the vampire mythos, with both vampires initially depicted as human beings and not undead fiends in human garb. Never have movies, at least not since the silent *Nosferatu*, depicted vampires as being so unlike the living. Later in the movie, the resurrected vampire sister Lucy (Carol Marsh) becomes the woman-in-white predator wandering the woods for child victims. She approaches her little sister Tania (Janina Faye) slowly and methodically, trying to smile as though she were happy to see her little sister, but Lucy finds her bloodlust difficult to hide, as well as her huge fangs. As she implores Tania to give her a big hug, the glowing metal crucifix held erect by Van Helsing (Peter Cushing) enters the frame and plunges forward, causing Lucy to grimace and breathe deliberately in almost orgasmic effort. When his holy relic touches the vampire's forehead, Lucy screams and the cross leaves a burned imprint in her ungodly flesh. The good doctor then forces the vampire to return to her underground tomb.

**Christopher Lee, carrying his bride Valerie Gaunt, in the dramatic library sequence from *Horror of Dracula***

**Mindless zombies from *Night of the Living Dead***

*Horror of Dracula* offered lush color photography and period set decorations. The acting is exemplary and the script and direction exciting. Hammer Film Productions were at their creative peak. But what makes *Horror of Dracula* resonate is this visual look of the unholy undead that entices, seduces and terrifies us. In pivotal sequences Count Dracula appears at Lucy's window and enters more as Lucy's lover than her murderer. He caresses and nuzzles her cheeks tenderly. Such foreplay is very much enjoyed by Lucy as is registered by her sly smile and lustful anticipation. In a similar sequence, Lee enters the bedroom of the more mature Mina (Melissa Stribling) and smiles at her as she walks backwards toward the bed, on which she collapses as the romantic Count plunges downward. Never has the

Judith O'Dea and Duane Jones from *Night of the Living Dead*

cult of the undead been depicted in such blatant sexual terms and never has the seduction of the innocent meant so much in horror film cinema.

The decade of the 1960s now allows for our ninth groundbreaking horror film entry, George Romero's *Night of the Living Dead*, a film important in many different ways. For instance, the acceptability of low-budget and independently released horror movies could now stand side-by-side with mainstream Hollywood output. And as the next decades were to demonstrate, the independently produced horror production would rule supreme. While the vampire was not replaced, *Night of the Living Dead* introduced the flesh-devouring zombie as primary monster of the modern era, a monster who still reigns today. The violence in *Night of the Living Dead* might seem fairly tame now, but back in 1968 never had mainstream cinema showed animated corpses biting into tender flesh and ripping tendons, muscle and flesh. And the film introduced monsters that yanked out vital living organs and chewed them up. Since the 1960s introduced the concept of anti-hero, *Night of the Living Dead* toyed with the concept of featuring an African American, Duane Jones, as the major hero, and then having him die violently at the hands of his saviors in the final minutes of the movie. When Duane Jones is shot through the head and killed instantly, his body thrown on the bonfire of fiery zombie flesh, jaws are dropping in movie theaters. The movie ends with humans making a comeback and the zombies retreating; however, the outcome of which species will eventually win is uncertain, and never has a horror film ended with such an ambivalent finale suggesting that zombies are down for the short term but not out for the long. George Zomero's use of locals to play the zombies gives the production a back home feel, and the use of so many exterior locations is a boon. *Night of the Living Dead* sets out to shock, and so many sequences deliver upon that promise. Perhaps the most shocking one, besides the ending, is when cute little Karen Cooper (Kyra Schon) dies and returns zombified and takes a garden spade to her mother, killing the unsuspecting adult with cruel determination. George Romero's cinematography and tone make *Night of the Living Dead* appear to be almost a documentary acted out by semi-professional actors, all unknowns, who could literally be our neighbors. For low-budget filmmaking, *Night of the Living Dead* is cutting edge and groundbreaking in many ways.

Mario Bava's *Black Sunday*, our tenth groundbreaker, introduced Italian horror to American audiences, even though it was not the first Italian horror film produced. A year earlier Georges Franju's *Eyes Without a Face* reached American shores re-cut and re-dubbed as *The Horror Chamber of Dr. Faustus*, yet that French horror film classic did not resonate with the American public in the same way as *Black Sunday*. For one thing, Mario Bava was about to

Barbara Steele, as the evil vampiric witch, is about to be burned at the stake in *Black Sunday*.

*Black Sunday* explores a new Euro vampire mythology.

the forthcoming decade. While Italian horror followed British horror as the third international horror arena because of the success of *Black Sunday*, such success only opened other international arenas to the horror film genre (Spain, France, etc.). *Black Sunday* introduced the world to Mario Bava, and the director became a star in his own right.

While American-International introduced the teenage drive-in sub-genre during the 1950s, the 1970s introduced the independent producer's teenage exploitation horror movie, its principal success arriving in 1978 with John Carpenter's *Halloween*, our eleventh groundbreaker. True, George Romero opened the door for independent productions in 1968, but Carpenter's *Halloween* became the highest grossing independent production of all time when first released. But *Halloween* introduced so much more. The era of teenage sexual abandonment was upon us, and we were on the cusp of AIDS. Movies such as *Halloween* created the premise that sex equals death. Those teens who indulge die. Virginal babysitter Jamie Lee Curtis fights the Shape of evil, Michael Myers, and survives. The era of the slasher movie was upon us, and no longer would human stars such as Karloff and Lugosi rule the horror film genre. Now the psychopathic killer would be the new horror movie icon—Michael Myers, Leatherface, Jason Voorhees and Fred Krueger. Unlike Alfred Hitchcock's *Psycho*, the slashers that *Halloween* introduced were nondescript human beings who wear some type of mask or who had their facial features mutilated. They were the sick psychos dressed in drag as *mother* without the Nor-

find most of his new films to be American released, and his name and talent would attract a cult following. Bava was a marvelous visual director and his personal stamp appeared on all his work, but *Black Sunday* offered the birth of a non-American horror film auteur. And the simple fact that *Black Sunday* was not American, that it was produced in Italy starring a mostly Italian cast, introduced the concept that horror films did not always have to be American and that the international arena of horror movies offered stylistic differences that demonstrated new artistic approaches to fright cinema. *Black Sunday* used vampire cinema as a hook to attract American audiences, but the simple fact that Bava created his own mythos of the undead showed that non-English language films did not have to follow the rules of American Universal or British Hammer to be creative or successful. *Black Sunday* introduced the concept of vampires as reincarnated witches and demons that could be destroyed with a metal spike through the eye. And Mario Bava's background as a brilliant cinematographer only imbued this film with a dazzling sense of style… slow-motion carriage shots, forests bathed in fog, fiends who disappear behind ornate fireplaces, etc. Bava and *Black Sunday* introduced the most leisurely European pacing and increased emphasis on mood to the American horror movie audience, in this case favoring mood over plot. And with the introduction of Barbara Steele to American audiences, *Black Sunday* introduced the concept of horror film queen to modern audiences, a sensual female entity that the Euro horror film would further embrace in

P.J. Soles, Nancy Loomis and Jamie Lee Curtis as the girls of *Halloween*

**The demon child possessed *The Exorcist***

man Bates human underbelly. The fiends were reduced of their humanity and become killing machines that often took on supernatural overtones (Michael Myers become the Shape who could never die; Jason became the hockey mask-wearing fiend who also could never be destroyed; Fred Krueger was dead but lived on in teenage nightmares). These human monsters were described in these movies as pure evil and they could never be defeated because evil itself exists and cannot be destroyed. Such horror film icons become personifications of evil energy. *Halloween* started the entire slasher influence in American cinema (copied and made more commercially successful by the *Friday the 13th* franchise), the scream queen and sexually provocative victim following closely behind. The focus was once again on the world of the young and most of the action occurs from teens' points of view. *Halloween* helped to introduce the body count movie to American audiences and it influenced many movies of inferior ilk to follow in its wake. *Halloween* was good moviemaking, but the films it directly influenced were often quick-buck cash-ins. The type of movie *Halloween* awakened ruled the exploitation American cinema for a long, long time.

Of all 13 groundbreaking films presented here, the one I detest the most is one of the most essential, *The Exorcist*, William Friedkin's 1973 blockbuster hit, our twelfth groundbreaker. *The Exorcist* for me was everything horror movies should not be—bombastic, special effects-dominated, pretentious, profane and mainstream. It would seem that mainstream, big budget horror movies would be a boon to the genre, and in the hands of a stylish director such as William Friedkin we could always hope for the best. But *The Exorcist* stressed all the wrong things. Instead of subtle mood (which occurred infrequently) we have bombast (windows being smashed by broken human bodies and ungodly loud hospital medical tests) and gross-out shocks (dialogue such as "may you suck cocks in Hell"). The makeup and effects draw too much attention, and the visual of having a pre-teen (actually an older stunt double) masturbate with a crucifix was simply over the top. It seems as though Friedkin does not understand the heart and soul of horror cinema, but like a boy in a candy store, Warner Bros. gave him the budget without the needed discipline or lessons in what makes horror movies effective. But perhaps due to the superb Hollywood hype, *The Exorcist* became one of the biggest grossing movies of that year and proved that horror movies could be huge box office. Of course the struggling independent Hammer Film Productions was quickly put out of its misery by movies that had the budget but lacked the soul to produce quality horror. To this day *The Exorcist* bores me and has me shaking my head in disbelief. Perhaps the classics *Alien* and *Aliens* might not have been made if it were not for *The Exorcist*, and for this one point we can be eternally grateful. But horror's reliance on makeup and gross-out effects comes directly from this film and horror cinema is still paying the price. Val Lewton proved that horror classics could be produced on a budget relying on the strength of talented writers, cinematographers and directors. Universal proved that eccentric, cutting-edge filmmaking could ignite the horror genre. Hammer proved, once again, that talent and tender loving care could compensate for a low budget. *The Exorcist* caught filmgoers' attention in the

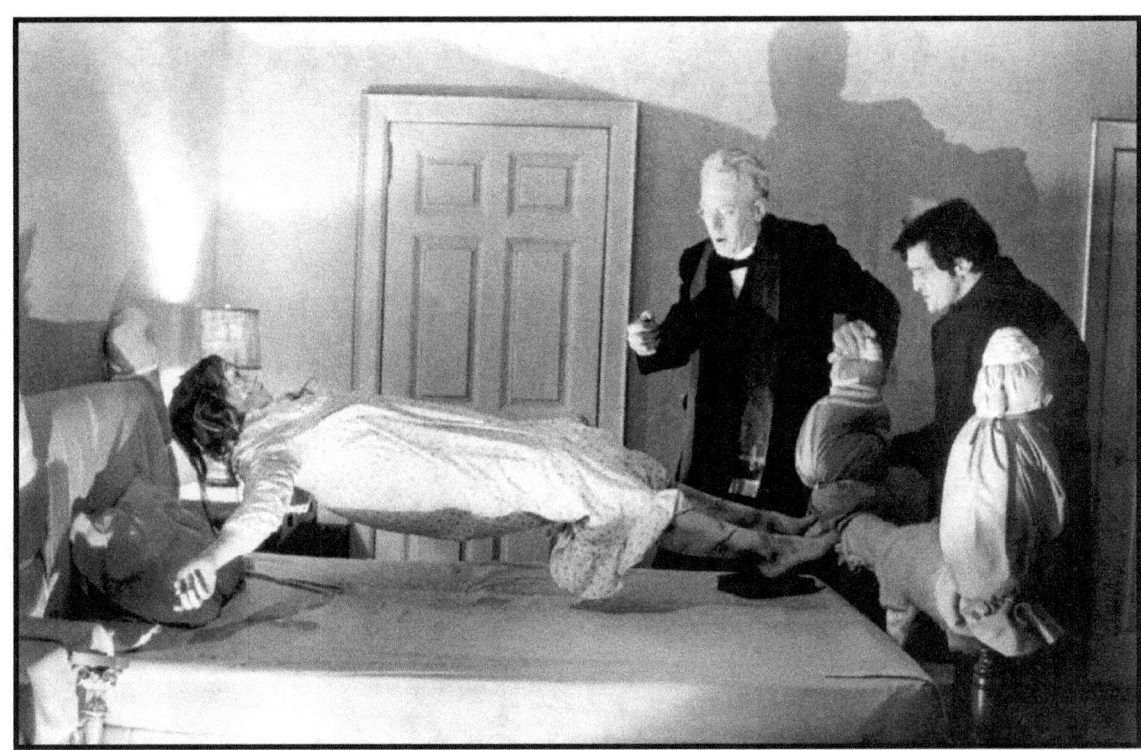
**The climatic exorcism conducted by Max Von Sydow and Jason Miller from *The Exorcist*.**

worst sense, but the movie's reliance on shock value with very little atmospheric chills only attests to the simple fact that *The Exorcist* both inspired and almost destroyed horror cinema for decades to come. If it were not for the Euro-trash entries and the slew of American independents produced during the 1970s, the horror film, like the Western, may have burned out creatively before our eyes.

Forget the decade of the 1980s, horror cinema's worst decade ever.

In the late 1990s Japanese horror cinema (labeled J-horror) reminded horror movie fans what truly mattered—a well-written script, emotion-based performances, atmospheric creeps and slowly building shocks. *Ringu* (*The Ring*), our final and thirteenth groundbreaker, took a while for Americans to catch up to since its release here arrived without fanfare or a wide release. It wasn't until America decided to remake Japanese horror classics such as *Ringu* and *Ju-On* (*The Grudge*) that American remade versions of the Japanese originals reached mainstream multiplexes. While most of these Japanese horror movies feature ghosts in many different shapes and forms, their critical acclaim encouraged directors to return to the atmospheric shocks of classic horror cinema, turning away from the gross-out shocks of big-budgeted movies such as *The Exorcist*. Such Japanese horror films influenced other Asian nations to follow suit (Hong Kong with *The Eye* and *Eye II* and Chinese horror, which predated Japanese, was now being rediscovered on home video and in art houses). If for no other reason than demonstrating that the creepy movies watched behind fingers-covering-the face could be audience crowd pleasers, these Japanese movies deserve a great deal of credit. In an era of an over-abundance of sex, nudity and profanity, these Japanese horror movies did not feature nudity, graphic sex or profanity. Instead such films merely creeped us out with visual imagery that long lingered in our mind's eye. Not since movies such as *Black Sunday* and *Black Sabbath* have directors rediscovered the slow-building chill that resonates and leaks under our skins, making the audience uneasy and eager to scream to find cathartic release. And such a reliance on good scripts and atmospheric horror has influenced many horror movies produced in the wake of movies such as *Ringu*.

So here's my list of the 13 most influential horror movies ever produced, movies that in themselves pushed the creativity of the horror film genre forward. These movies may have been influenced by the past but they were never simply repeating past glories. Such groundbreaking movies were always challenging the movie audience by daring to terrify us in new, original ways. But as I said at the start, I only allowed myself 13 movies, so if readers want to make a case for dropping one or more titles and adding a few different choices, I would be eager to hear divergent points of view. The best ones will be published.

The 13 most influencial horror movies once again!
*Frankenstein; The Black Cat; King Kong; Frankenstein Meets the Wolf Man; Cat People; The Thing; I Was a Teenage Werewolf; Horror of Dracula; Night of the Living Dead; Black Sunday; Halloween; The Exorcist; Ringu*

# LUGOSI VS. KARLOFF—ETERNALLY!
### by Gary D. Rhodes

Some months ago, when I first decided to write about Universal's DVD set *The Bela Lugosi Collection*, my plans were pretty clear. Examine the films, and, in general, enjoy the fact that three of the five movies in the set are completely new to DVD and all of them are new to NTSC Region 1. But the weeks leading up to the *BL Collection's* September 6, 2005 release date changed that idea of mine a fair bit, as the DVD set has quickly become one of the most controversial classic horror home video releases in history.

The context is one that reaches back nearly 75 years, of course. Horror fans know the story note and verse, but sometimes disagree on whether to play it in a major or minor key. After scoring in *Dracula* (1931), Bela Lugosi turned down the part of the Monster in what became James Whale's 1931 classic *Frankenstein* (or he was eased out by Whale, as the story has also been told?).

Karloff's success meant that in 1932 Universal clearly announced its intention to make him a star. And that meant Lugosi was less on their radar screen (or they were out to get him, as the most hardened Lugosi defenders claim). At any rate, Karloff generally got more attention, better parts and better pay; he also got top billing over Lugosi when they appeared together onscreen.

As the years wore on, Karloff's career always fared better than Lugosi's, with the latter occasionally forced to follow grudgingly in the former's footsteps. In 1943, Lugosi finally did appear as the Frankenstein Monster in *Frankenstein Meets the Wolf Man*, as well as taking on the stage role of Jonathan Brewster in *Arsenic and Old Lace* (the role originally created on Broadway by Karloff).

At the end of his life in the mid-1950s, Lugosi still bore a grudge. By contrast, Karloff dubbed his former co-star "Poor Bela," a phrase that, while born out of apparent sympathy, continues to anger many Lugosi fans as being condescending.

After Lugosi's 1956 death, Karloff's presence in the media actually increased thanks to TV, films, record albums and new cultural landmarks like *How the Grinch Stole Christmas!* (1966). Readers of *Famous Monsters of Filmland* were told that "Lugosi Lives Eternal!" but his compatriot in horror was "King Karloff." He was the gentle soul behind horror classics, whereas Lugosi was the typecast vampire whose fate became Poverty Row horror films, Ed Wood and narcotics.

The tide began to turn in the 1980s, partly as a backlash against the "Karloff is better" stance held by some, but also out of a genuine interest in Lugosi's work and an emergent scholarly effort to understand his place in film history.

Critical reception of Lugosi's lower-budget films improved, his memorabilia became far more valuable than ever and fan clubs, newsletters and books appeared throughout the late 1980s and '90s. More than anything else, a perceived victory over Karloff came with Martin Landau's Academy-Award winning portrayal of Lugosi in Tim Burton's *Ed Wood* (1994).

But of course, this is just one way of telling the story. After all, original movie posters for Karloff's *Frankenstein* (1931) and *The Mummy* (1932) have taken a lot more money at auction than Lugosi's *Dracula* (1931). More than one important book on Karloff has been published in recent years. And even if only a cameo, Jack Betts appeared as Karloff in Bill Condon's *Gods and Monsters* (1998).

All of the past is prologue to the current debacle, a "Lugosi Collection" in which only one film (*Murder in the Rue Morgue* of 1932) headlines Lugosi. The other four films (*The Black Cat* of 1934, *The Raven* of 1935, *The Invisible Ray* of 1936 and *Black Friday* of 1940) all co-star Lugosi with Karloff—with Karloff top-billed in all their pairings.

Karloff's daughter Sara was quoted on one horror film site as saying, "This is a missed opportunity. These are very good films and it is a missed opportunity [to release these films] as collaborations." Her attitude that both Lugosi and Karloff's names should appear on the packaging was a view echoed in many quarters of film fandom.

**Boris Karloff and Bela Lugosi, circa 1932**

By all accounts, many fans wrote to Universal with complaints and certainly aired their discontent at great length on the web. King Karloff had been dethroned by the same Universal Studios that had for decades favored him over Lugosi, but why? Some horror buffs were insulted; others were simply puzzled.

Could it be that the tide had really turned so much toward Lugosi that the studio believed it was his name and his name alone that would sell DVDs? Had *Ed Wood* (1994) and other Lugosi projects generated such a huge and ongoing fan base?

Maybe, but maybe not. Rumors have also spread about Sara Karloff's business difficulties with Universal Studios. Out of retribution or simple economy perhaps, the studio turned to the Lugosi-only strategy. Despite Bela Lugosi, Jr.'s lawsuits against Universal in years past, the son of Dracula currently has a good relationship with the studio. Paying one heir licensing fees instead of two may have prompted the decision. And it might not have been hard for Universal to choose which heir was most cooperative.

Regardless of the reason, though, Karloff's name isn't on the DVD cover and you have to squint to see a small picture of him on the back of the box. The only other image of Karloff anywhere to be found is a still from *The Invisible Ray*, an image hidden by the DVD itself until you remove it from its hub.

Speculation on the Internet has also prompted hopes that it would just be a matter of time before Universal would release a *Boris Karloff Collection*. But that guess seems undercut by the reality that the only Karloff Universals not already on DVD just aren't of the same caliber as those on the *Lugosi Collection*. True, we have *Tower of London* (1939), but the others (*Night Key* of 1937, *The Climax* of 1944, *The Strange Door* of 1951 and *The Black Castle* of 1952) aren't at all beloved by the whole of horror fandom, let alone known to the wider population of DVD customers.

Short of crafting a collection from those films, the company could release *The Miracle Man* (1932), a Paramount they own, in which Karloff has a minor role. Or they could issue *Scarface* (1932), an eagerly awaited DVD release to be sure, but one in which Karloff has only a small part. And—like *The Miracle Man*—it certainly isn't a horror film, which if placed in a *BK Collection* would be a bit odd, but maybe no more odd than what's happened with this Lugosi set.

At any rate, all of this meant that the weeks leading up to the September 2005 release of the *BL Collection*

Another early 1930s publicity shot of Boris Karloff and Bela Lugosi

were mired in controversy. And as soon as the DVD made its way into collectors' hands, new problems arose. Reports of playback problems spread on the Internet like wildfire. Many viewers have detected problems at about 21, 30, and/or 35 minutes into *The Raven* that causes the image to freeze or even jump to the next chapter. Others have had problems with *The Black Cat* freezing at about 24 minutes in. Similar issues have been experienced with *Black Friday*.

All these troubles seem traceable to Universal's decision to squeeze five feature films onto one DVD-18 disc, which led Dave Kerr at the *New York Times* (September 2, 2005) to dub the *Lugosi Collection* "the first single-disc box set in history," adding "All that crowding means a lot of video compression." One member of the online Classic Horror Film Board was even less kind in describing what he perceived as "a home video catastrophe." Rather than authoring defects per se, it seems that many DVD players are simply having difficulties with DVD-18. Moving past the overall question of playback (which, granted, is a hard one to move past), we can at least enjoy the fact that, when the disc does play properly, none of these films has ever looked better. Along with much cleaner picture and audio than the junky 16mm prints shown on TV and some film festivals in years passed, the quality on each film trumps all prior home video releases.

Whether it is remembering the original and quite awful first video release of *The Black Cat* and *The Raven* as a dual 1984 VHS release and laserdisc release that altered their speeds, their much better individual releases on VHS in the 1990s, or (perhaps worst-of-all) their overly soft picture quality on Magna Pacific's PAL Region 2 DVD (packaged as a "Boris Karloff Triple Feature" with *The Mummy* [1932])—well, it is hard to imagine ever seeing these two films look and sound better than they do now.

The same could be said of *Murders in the Rue Morgue*, *Invisible Ray* and *Black Friday*. In particular the audio quality of *Rue Morgue* sounds so much crisper than ever before.

And what about the films themselves? After the more obvious Universal monsters (*Dracula*, *Frankenstein*, *The Mummy*, *The Wolf Man*), these films represent some of the best works of the Golden Age of horror films, a key reason why their presentation has raised so much ire.

Presented chronologically (and with menu screens featuring images of Lugosi without Karloff), the first three films are all based on the works of Edgar Allan Poe. Arriving in the early 1930s when U.S. scholarship on the author was increasing, this trio of films offers little of Poe beyond his story titles.

But the Poe films do illustrate what was already happening in the 1930s U.S. horror film. Consciously or not, *Dracula*, *Frankenstein*, *The Mummy* and others attempted to Americanize horror. Even if the villain lurking was clearly coded as non-American, he was an intruder into an increasingly American tale. For example, these films featured largely American actors portraying what were supposed to be European characters (Helen Chandler, Edward Van Sloan, Dwight Frye, Mae Clarke). The character name "Victor" Frankenstein was changed to "Henry." Tod Browning's used an armadillo in *Dracula*, an image of horror stemming certainly from the American Southwest, not Transylvania. The use of Poe storylines (or at least referencing them by title) was another form of this, drawing as it did on the work of an American author.

That said, *Murders in The Rue Morgue* is Poe's detective story twisted into a horror tale that tapped into a particularly U.S. tension between science and religion. *Murders in the Rue Morgue* explored the conflict over the same evolutionary principles that resulted in the Scopes Monkey Trial of the 1920s right alongside rape, prostitution and bestiality. When it was eleased in early 1932, director Robert Florey crafted a film almost as challenging to audience sensibilities as Tod Browning's *Freaks*, which was simultaneously playing many U.S. theaters.

Of course, the film has had an uneasy position in horror film history. Most fans applaud Lugosi's performance and the set design while bashing just about everything else. And to be sure, the film does have shortcomings, created in part at least by the studio's re-edit of the film (described by Tim Lucas in *Video Watchdog*).

Even with its being the one non-Karloff film in this set, Karloff seems to hover over it, as Lugosi was cast in *Rue Morgue* when Karloff took on the role of the Monster in *Frankenstein*. Interesting too that Lugosi's character Dr. Mirakle—an obsessed mad scientist attempting to create new life by relying on the bodies of several women—is to a degree a rethinking of Colin Clive's doctor in *Frankenstein,* just as Universal's *The Mummy* (1932) was a semi-remake of *Dracula* (1931). Had Lugosi been able to play Dr. Frankenstein instead of the Monster, he almost certainly would have tried to stay attached to the Whale film. At the least, *Rue Morgue* gives us a peek at how he may have approached the role.

Despite its bad reputation, *Murders in the Rue Morgue* is ripe for a reappraisal even without considering *Frankenstein*. Just as it did better with many critics and audiences in 1932 than historians have generally acknowledged, it plays better now than some modern writers admit.

Though it doesn't fulfill the promise of Florey's 1928 short *The Life of 9413, a Hollywood Extra* (released in August 2005 as part of Kino's two-DVD set *Avant Garde—Experimental Cinema of the 1920s & 1930s*), *Rue Morgue* features an Expressionist *mise-en-scene* unmatched by any other 1930s horror film. And if it creaks a bit with age, it creaks with the same kind of spookiness as a squeaky door in an old house.

By contrast, *The Black Cat* seems quite modern thanks to its set design and fast pacing. And even more overtly than *Murders in the Rue Morgue*, Edgar Ulmer's *The Black Cat* explores taboo subjects, featuring themes of incest, Satanism and a climax in which Lugosi's Dr. Werdegast literally skins Karloff's Hjalmar Poelzig alive.

The 1930s horror film often addressed fears of modernity by showing just how awful science and technology could be. Of course the most famous examples of this, films like *Frankenstein*

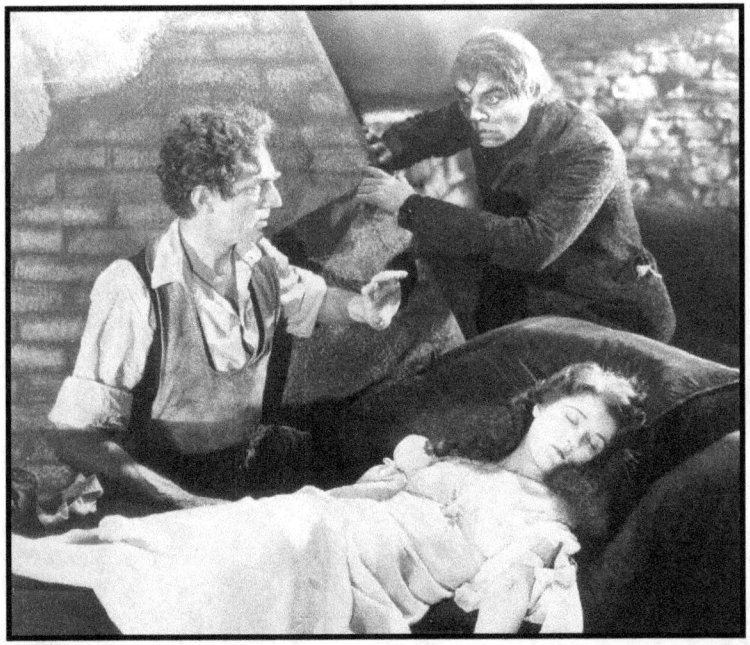

**Bela Lugosi, Noble Johnson and Sydney Fox from *Murders in the Rue Morgue***

Karloff and Lugosi strike a sinister pose in *The Black Cat*.

and physical existence, in some ways as inexplicable and awful as that suffered by the narrator of a short story like "The Pit and the Pendulum."

In the end, *The Black Cat* seems to be a draw between Karloff and Lugosi in terms of the juicy roles they were both given and the merits of their own performances. Karloff's name, though, still came first in the billing.

In *The Raven*, though, Lugosi clearly wins the day in terms of his screen time and the extreme latitude he gives to his character Dr. Vollin, perhaps the maddest doctor of the 1930s. There's also more Edgar Allan here than in the prior two films, with Vollin reciting bits of the title poem and being generally obsessed with all things Poe.

Vollin wasn't just the wildest, most maniacal characterization Lugosi would ever create. His power over Karloff's Bateman character makes this one a favorite for Lugosi fans. Lugosi later outshined Karloff in *Son of Frankenstein* (1939, released in 2004 in Universal's *Frankenstein—The Legacy* collection), but in it he was still a member of an ensemble cast that included actors like

and *Bride of Frankenstein*, sometimes explored these themes in stories set in an earlier time period. The present invaded the past with terrible results.

*The Black Cat* is an inversion of that formula. The story clearly takes place in the 1930s, the time period in which it was made. Modernity is witnessed not only by automobiles, but also famously by the ultra-modern design of Poelzig's home. And here the past encroaches horrifically upon the present.

This happens not just in the planned revenge of Werdegast on Poelzig, but in a larger and even more eerie sense. Satanism and the black mass of a distant past slink uneasily into contemporary life in the same way real-life Aleister Crowley had surfaced into 20th-century popular media. Behind the walls of even a forward-looking house were eyes that gazed into age-old evil.

Though the roaming black cat seems forced into the plot to justify the title, Lugosi's character contains a quality that actually seems very evocative of Poe's work. Werdegast has endured a tortured mental

Basil Rathbone and Lionel Atwill. In *The Raven*, Lugosi was able to dominate every element of the film, including Karloff.

But for the actor, this was a hollow victory, not merely because Karloff once again got top billing. The extreme antics of Dr. Vollin placed Lugosi further than ever from the kind of roles he craved. The same year as *The Raven*, Lugosi tried to get a production company off the ground to change all that. A lack of funding meant nothing came of it, and he remained trapped in the world of horror.

*The Invisible Ray* is notable not so much as a science fiction film (after all, the bulk of the horror films of the 1930s were science fiction—mad doctors on the loose, meddling in pursuits best left alone), but as one of the closing chapters of the 1930s horror genre. "Uncle Carl" Laemmle would soon sell the studio, and a British ban on horror films would take them off the production schedule till late 1938. Given that Lugosi didn't get to appear in *Dracula's Daughter* (1936), he would disappear from horror films after *Invisible Ray* until *Son of Frankenstein* (1939) ignited another genre cycle from 1939-45.

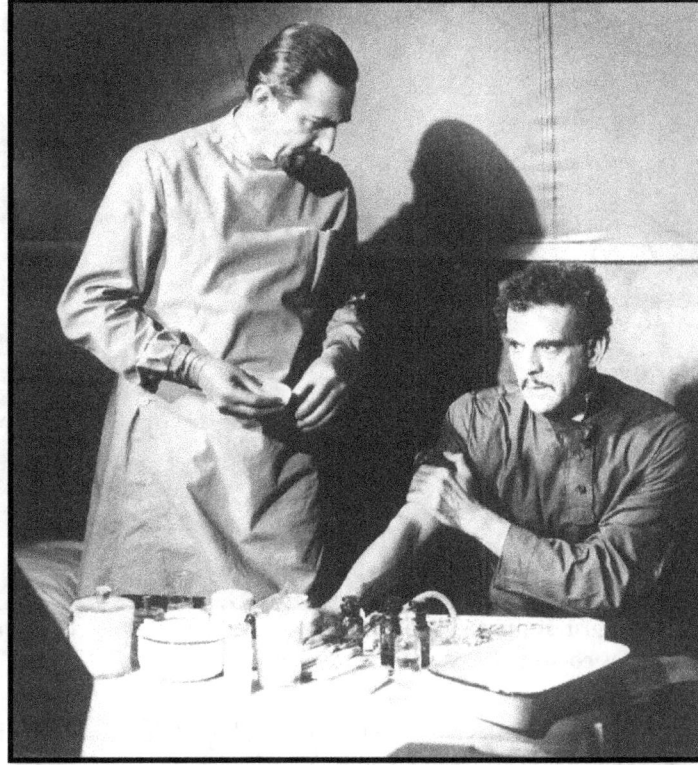

**Dr. Benet (Lugosi) and Rukh (Karloff) in *The Invisible Ray***

Watching *The Invisible Ray* now highlights how much Karloff and Lugosi's respective situation had changed since *The Black Cat* of just two years before. As Dr. Rukh, Karloff gets not only more screen time than he did as Poelzig, but a more complex character with more depth. As Dr. Benet, Lugosi is again playing a sympathetic character, but one without the depth, back story or screen time that he had as Werdegast.

And to say that Karloff gets top billing again would actually understate the conditions that prevailed; in words alone it is hard to describe how much the size of his name graphically dominated the film's posters and press materials.

But it's *Black Friday*, the last film in this set, that's perhaps the most curious entry in the *BL Collection*. Watching *Black Friday*, we see that it truly is a Karloff film in which Lugosi briefly appears. Even a mention of the picture causes some Lugosi buffs to bristle, as this turn of events of course didn't have to be. After all, Lugosi was supposed to play Karloff's Dr. Sovac role, but he was bumped to the small role of Eric Marnay, a part that greatly limited screen time, none of which was shared with Karloff.

At the same time, *Black Friday* is fascinating because it reunited Lugosi with Arthur Lubin, who had directed him in the his first Broadway play, *The Red Poppy* (1922). His part as a gangster, however tiny, is a departure from his standard horror film roles. And though he was billed below Karloff, it is key to remember that Lugosi was allegedly hypnotized to make one of his scenes more realistic. Even if he really wasn't (as he later confessed to friends), the stunt garnered him far more publicity than Karloff received.

Bela Lugosi supposedly being hypnotized on the set of *Black Friday* as co-star Boris Karloff looks on.

In the end, of course all five movies are a highly welcome addition to DVD regardless of their packaging. A more worthwhile groan than the box cover might actually be given in response to the overall lack of extra features. No audio commentaries, and certainly no documentary film. Even some basic historical footage isn't present. Newsreel footage exists of Karloff and Lugosi judging felines for *The Black Cat*, but it isn't here. Nor is their riff on *The Black Cat* chess game in the short subject *Screen Snapshots 11* (1934).

No trailers for *The Black Cat* or *The Raven*, either. This isn't as much a surprise, since Universal simply didn't make film trailers in the early 1930s; those that were made were farmed out to trailer companies like National Screen Service and (as in the case of the original *Dracula* and *Frankenstein* trailers) don't seem to have been archived at Universal. A shame, since trailer companies were often given alternate takes from those used in the final release versions of films and sometimes even cut shots/scenes.

But to be fair, it isn't as if the disc's optional French and Spanish subtitles are all that the folks at Universal saw fit to give us. We should at least be very thankful for the trailer for *Black Friday*, which is the original even if it bears a Realart reissue logo. The running time emphasizes Lugosi and shows what is likely the only existing on-the-set footage of the actor being hypnotized (an event also covered in one newsreel of the time that seems to be lost).

Reissue trailers for *Murders in the Rue Morgue* and *Invisible Ray* are here also, with the former one sporting beautiful font styles, bad editing and strains of *Swan Lake* that very much seems to indicate it was used in 1932 and later recycled by Realart.

So very little in the way of extras for five feature films selling for under 20 bucks on a single disc that is causing some customers trouble. It's hard to know whether to celebrate or complain, to toast a drink or to get dead drunk.

Adding my own two cents to the controversies, I wished for a second or third DVD to allow room for the other remaining Lugosi films in the Universal catalogue. Even if they had eschewed their now-public domain *Postal Inspector* (1936, available on Alpha DVD) and *The Phantom Creeps* serial and/or feature (1939, available as a serial on Alpha DVD), I think of the films now less likely than ever to make it to DVD without being part of a "collection": *Gift of Gab* (1934, with Lugosi and Karloff), *The Black Cat* (1941, with Lugosi, Basil Rathbone, and Gale Sondergaard) and *Night Monster* (1942, with Lugosi and Lionel Atwill).

Our best hope now is that Universal will soon release the much better known *Island of Lost Souls* (1932), a Paramount film of Lugosi's that they own (as is the case with the W.C. Fields–Lugosi film *International House* [1933], released on DVD by Universal in their 2004 *W.C. Fields Comedy Collection*). But maybe we won't be so lucky; Amazon.com strangely lists the film as a DVD slated for the year 2010!

As for the present set, the absence of Karloff's name on the box certainly won't affect the onscreen film credits or history books that record his top-billed status.

On the other hand, in the short term at least, it seems Lugosi's name will continue to trump Karloff's in the world at large. No major Karloff projects seem to in the offing, but several on Lugosi are underway. I'm at work on two Lugosi books myself, one of which will be published in 2006.

And most fascinating of all, the revised and expanded edition of Gregory Mank's *Karloff and Lugosi: The Story of a Haunting Collaboration* (McFarland, 1988) will not only be published soon, but will sport a new title... *Lugosi and Karloff!*

So along with everything else, the *BL Collection* highlights how the chess pieces have moved since Karloff and Lugosi played that game in *The Black Cat*. I am reminded that somewhere in recent cyberspace, one horror film fan dubbed a new phrase: "Poor Boris." But what with all the compression troubles on the *Lugosi Collection*, maybe it should really be "Poor KARLOFF and Bela (Dracula) Lugosi."

—Gary D. Rhodes is the author of *Lugosi* (McFarland, 1997) and *White Zombie: Anatomy of a Horror Film* (McFarland, 2001), as well as the writer/director of the documentary film *Lugosi: Hollywood's Dracula*.

# Forum/Against 'Em

### Edited by Anthony Ambrogio

## The Wolf Man

I always thought *The Wolf Man* (1941) was one of horror cinema's sacred cows (if you'll pardon the mixed metaphor), but that's because I didn't reckon on the critical wrath of *Midnight Marquee*'s esteemed editor and publisher Gary J. Svehla (**Gary** below). Yet another round of *Forum/Against 'Em* begins—innocently enough—with a passing remark by Bruce Dettman (**Bruce**), who has written for *Midnight Marquee* and who writes about the 1950s *Superman* TV series and other filmic matters (e.g., variations on the gunfight at the OK Corral). Bruce's comment was enough to spark Gary's surprisingly negative critique (who knew he felt this way?), which he defends against all comers—all comers including frequent *MidMar* contributor Steven Thornton (**Steve**), whose "Sounds of Silents" graced the pages of the 40th anniversary issue (*Midnight Marquee* 69/70 [2003]); author Mark Clark (**Mark**), whose book *Smirk, Sneer, and Scream* was nominated for a 2004 Rondo Award; Brian Smith, whose fine writing on "The Three Faces of Dracula" can be found elsewhere in this issue; and yours truly, Anthony Ambrogio (**Anthony**), who always seems to be editing these things. Oh, and Arthur Lundquist (**Arthur**), whose recent *Midnight Marquee* contribution was "2001's Cinematic Relativity" for issue 71/72, chimed in for a couple of comments, too.

**Bruce:** I loved *The Wolf Man* (1941) as a kid. I can still hear my mother screaming at me through my locked bedroom door: "No turning into the Wolf Man until your homework is done!" But, as I grew older, my affection waned a bit. I found something forced and perhaps heavy-handed about it. Of late, however, I've begun to drift toward it again. Not certain why.

**Gary:** *The Wolf Man* is absolutely mediocre. I like the film more now than I did as a youngster, but the film generally lacks a sense of pacing and dread. Lon Chaney is not horrible, but he's bland and very self-conscious, making the viewer aware of the artifice of his acting. Yes, the final forest scenes, draped in fog, are wonderful. But over an hour of the movie lacks emotional involvement and meanders. The film's major flaw is its lack of directorial style and atmosphere. Maria Ouspenskaya and Bela Lugosi are wonderful, but the rest of the cast is okay at best.

*Frankenstein Meets the Wolf Man* (1943), though a monster rally and a B production, creates more mood and dread in its opening graveyard sequence when the lycanthrope revives than *The Wolf Man* does in its entirety. The Wolf Man is a fantastic-looking monster, but the movie is the reason why Universal gave up on its original A-production monster opuses and instead settled for B programmers that re-filtered the older monsters into kiddy fodder (wonderful kiddy fodder, but kiddy fodder nonetheless).

Any time anybody is ready to climb into the squared circle and have a forum/against-'em, no-disqualification match about *The Wolf Man*, I am ready.

**Steven:** Challenge issued and accepted!

Respectfully, Gary, I don't think a film that's merely mediocre could establish an enduring horror mythology. I agree that *The Wolf Man* has a number of flaws. The direction, for the most part, is pedestrian. The supporting cast

**Lon Chaney, Jr. as the Wolf Man, a fantastic-looking monster.**

outshines Chaney in nearly every scene. And the script has a connect-the-dots approach that feels like formula. (Given its early date, perhaps "boilerplate for formula" might be a more apt descriptor.)

**Gary:** First of all, Steven, I think the enduring aspects of the Wolf Man come *not* from the original film but from his appearances in *Frankenstein Meets the Wolf Man* and the monster-rally films *House of Frankenstein* (1944), *House of Dracula* (1945) and *Abbott & Costello Meet Frankenstein* (1948). I think the look and climax of the original film whetted viewers' appetites, and the sequels established the beast's legacy. Your stated flaws about *The Wolf Man* are insightful and spot on.

*The Wolf Man* is mediocre in every way.

**Mark:** I can only say, with affection and respect, that Gary must be off his nut to label *The Wolf Man* "mediocre." It's perhaps the only Universal film of the 1940s that can rival the studio's 1930s output as sheer visual poetry and for its lingering sense of dread.

*The Wolf Man* is a profoundly fatalistic film, which may turn off some viewers. Yet it remains a magnificent, archetypal film. So is *The Mummy* (1933)—which is at once the most romantic and most spiritual (in a defiantly non-Christian way) of all the Universal horror classics. It's a beautiful film in every respect, powered by one of Karloff's greatest performances (and, therefore, one of horror cinema's greatest performances).

**Gary:** Mark, you might be correct about me off my nut. But if that's the case, I've been that way for decades.

Sheer visual poetry is exactly what *The Wolf Man* lacks. Back in the pre-VCR mid-1970s when I was collecting film on reels, I was offered a gorgeous 16mm print of *The Wolf Man* and loaned the film for a week in order to decide. The print was pristine. I watched the movie twice and said, "God, this film is horrible—worse than I remember it on TV!" The price was sweet, but I passed on the purchase. Chaney always turned me off, but I would have ignored his self-conscious performance had the film had consistent directorial style and dramatic pacing. Besides the climax and one or two other short sequences, the film is bland. Even Evelyn Ankers, other than being nice to look at, is fair at best. Nothing, absolutely nothing, elevates the film to classic status except for the monster makeup, the film's climax in the woods and a few scenes with Maria Ouspenskaya. No, *Frankenstein Meets the Wolf Man* is faster-paced, more moody and stylish, and much superior to *The Wolf Man*. I won't beat a dead werewolf to death, but to me *The Wolf Man* has always been the most overrated horror-film "classic" ever made, and it underwhelms me every time I see it. I am *shocked* not that some people here like it, but that they consider it a classic.

**Anthony:** The depths of Gary's dislike for *The Wolf Man* distresses me. (Gary, is this critical payback for my denigration of *Bride of Frankenstein* [1935]?)

*The Wolf Man* is a nearly perfect story. It's an Aristotelian tragedy that practically follows the three unities of time, place and action. It boasts a superior cast and possesses a breakneck, relentless pace, full of subtle foreshadowings. (For example, Larry Talbot, coming on to Gwen Conliff in the antiques shop, shows himself to be a figurative *wolf* that then becomes a literal wolf.)

**Brian:** I absolutely agree with you here—Talbot is being a total wolf when he first meets Gwen in the antiques shop. I think that's the joke with the wolf-head cane that he purchases. Doesn't Gwen even say something like, "This one would be appropriate for you" when she's pointing out the wolf cane to him? I think there's a little knowing kind of reference like that in there.

**Anthony:** (She says the *dog*-head cane he first picks up would "suit" him—which may express her feelings about his unwanted attentions.)

**Steven:** As an aside, I find it interesting, and refreshing, to watch a Hollywood film in which a very average Joe gets to hit on an attractive woman. I don't think anyone really believes Larry stands a chance with Gwen Conliffe, but it gives hope to us less-than-studly guys that such things can indeed happen (if only in our heads!).

**Brian:** It's a tribute to the acting skill of Evelyn Ankers that she makes you believe that Gwen is actually attracted to this overbearing lug.

*The Wolf Man* **really nails the concept of a man cursed through no fault of his own. Chaney and Marie Ouspenskaya**

**Steven:** What *The Wolf Man* does well, it does very, very well. The elaborate and convincing bit of folklore invented by Siodmak fits the film superbly and lifts it a notch above most other horror films of the era. The visual of Chaney stalking Ankers through the woods is the stuff from which nightmares are made. And, most importantly, *The Wolf Man*, more than any other werewolf movie, really nails the concept of man cursed through no fault of his own. That's a very powerful mythos and one that arguably reflects real life more accurately than the 1931 *Frankenstein*'s man-playing-God allegory or the 1931 *Dracula*'s religious/sexual overtones.

**Gary:** True, the mythology of lycanthropy established by Curt Siodmak is more than a little responsible for the Wolf Man's enduring legacy as horror icon. All the points you make are strong, and ones with which I agree. But a moody and well-photographed climax (let's face it, the Wolf Man stalking Ankers in the woods is three minutes long at most) does not a classic make. Chaney's acting tends to undermine the concept of the character Siodmak created in the script. And that "acting" further undermines the classic aspects of what is showing itself to be, from our simple discussion, a more and more flawed movie. *The Wolf Man* has at best eight great minutes and more filler than any other A-production Universal horror movie. Siodmak's contribution is classic, but, as ultimately executed in the film—well, it's another case of a movie working better on paper.

*Frankenstein Meets the Wolf Man*, not *The Wolf Man*, established the enduring legacy of this classic Universal monster.

**Bela Lugosi as Bela the Gypsy**

**Mark:** To my mind, Gary, the only tradition that *Meets* established was that of the monster rally—which may or may not be a good thing, depending on your point of view. And, if any movie ever qualified for the label "mediocre," *Meets* would be the one. Other than the admittedly fine opening and the visual splendor of Ilona Massey, the film has little to offer to serious horror fans.

**Steven:** I don't want to be too unkind to *Frankenstein Meets the Wolf Man* because I know a lot of people are fond of it. But it seems to me that this is the film where Universal demonstrates an unflinching commitment to mediocrity and never looks back.

If imitation is any indication of success, the first werewolf copycat films that I can identify are *The Mad Monster* and *The Undying Monster*—both released in 1942, immediately after *The Wolf Man* and prior to *Meets*. I don't know if this is conclusive, but it suggests *The Wolf Man* is indeed the film that established an ongoing legacy. (I have no reference material on pulps and radio shows, but I'd be curious to know if a Wolf Man clone pops his furry little paws into either of those formats in mid-1942. Can anyone verify?)

**Anthony:** A cursory glance at the episode titles of the *I Love a Mystery* program for 1942 shows nothing that smacks of lycanthropy. A Plastic Man story published in *Police Comics* 26 (January 1944), "Body, Mind, and Soul!" features a werewolf.

**Mark:** If we're gonna talk about *Wolf Man* imitations, we can't forget to mention *Cat People* (also 1942).

**Anthony:** Shoot, Mark, *I* wanted to say that! Val Lewton's *Cat People*, another metamorphosis drama, *had* to be inspired by *The Wolf Man*—by its success and by the nature of its monster. One can argue for the superiority of the Lewton product (I wouldn't, in this instance), but one cannot deny *The Wolf Man*'s influence.

**Gary:** I'll admit that *The Wolf Man* did influence *Cat People* and other movies (such as *Cat Man of Paris* [1946]). But I'd argue that the major influence wasn't the movie itself but Jack Pierce's terrific monster conception. I consider *Cat People* one of the top 20 greatest horror movies ever produced. So I have to thank *The Wolf Man* for influencing a far greater production created in its wake.

**Anthony:** I'm sorry to read that Gary thinks there are only eight good minutes in *The Wolf Man*. It's a picture that has a forward narrative thrust, that tosses out exposition as it speeds along and lets the viewer pick it up and make of it what s/he will. Case in point: Larry returns to the ancestral home and chats with his father, awkwardly expressing, at the sight of his late brother's portrait, "I'm… sorry about John, father." We never learn much about the hunting accident that took Sir John's namesake's life—nor about the reasons for Sir John's mother taking Larry away to America for all those years, but we can speculate like crazy: It gives us the impression that (1) Sir John has been a tight-ass for a long time; (2) he is responsible for driving away his wife and young son; and (3)—who knows?—he may even have been responsible in some way for his first son's accidental death (a surmise that lends irony and further pathos to the end of the film). The fact that Larry is good with his hands and can fix a telescope leads directly to his voyeurism, spying on Gwen putting on her earrings, to his visit to the shop and all that Little Red Riding Hood/Big Bad Wolf banter. The Gypsies pass by, allowing Larry the opportunity to coerce Gwen into a date, and she turns the tables on him by bringing along a chaperone, Jenny. When Jenny has her fortune told, son Bela and mother Maleva exchange portentous looks; there's the business about the wolfbane which he flings off the table, and the reading culminates with the vision of the pentagram in her palm—all stuff that is unspoken, all contributing to the mood.

The thought of Claude Rains' Sir John being Lon Chaney, Jr.'s Lawrence's father is silly!

Later, after Larry has grappled with the wolf, killed it, and been carted home, someone says he was brought by the Gypsy woman, and—instead of a protracted and unnecessary "was-there-or-wasn't-there-someone-here" moment, Ralph Bellamy's Col. Montford impatiently cries, "Yes, yes," refers to Maleva's presence, and then they get on with tending to the business at hand.

It's stuff like this, including the busy-body gossip in the shop that Larry interrupts with a "No! Tell *me*!" and the scene where he cannot endure being in church—both because the eyes of the congregation are upon him and because something fundamental has changed inside him—that show what a superbly constructed picture *The Wolf Man* is.

**Gary:** Now Anthony is making me want to go back and watch *The Wolf Man* one more time to see if I get the same impressions. Drat!

**Anthony:** I am flattered if anything I might have written has caused Gary to want to go back and re-evaluate *The Wolf Man*.

I hope you do, Gary. I know that you may end up merely confirming your initial/on-going impression—but you never can tell.

**Mark:** Look for the visual poetry if you watch *The Wolf Man* again, Gary. Nothing in *The Wolf Man* looks quite

The fog-shrouded sets... poetic realism?

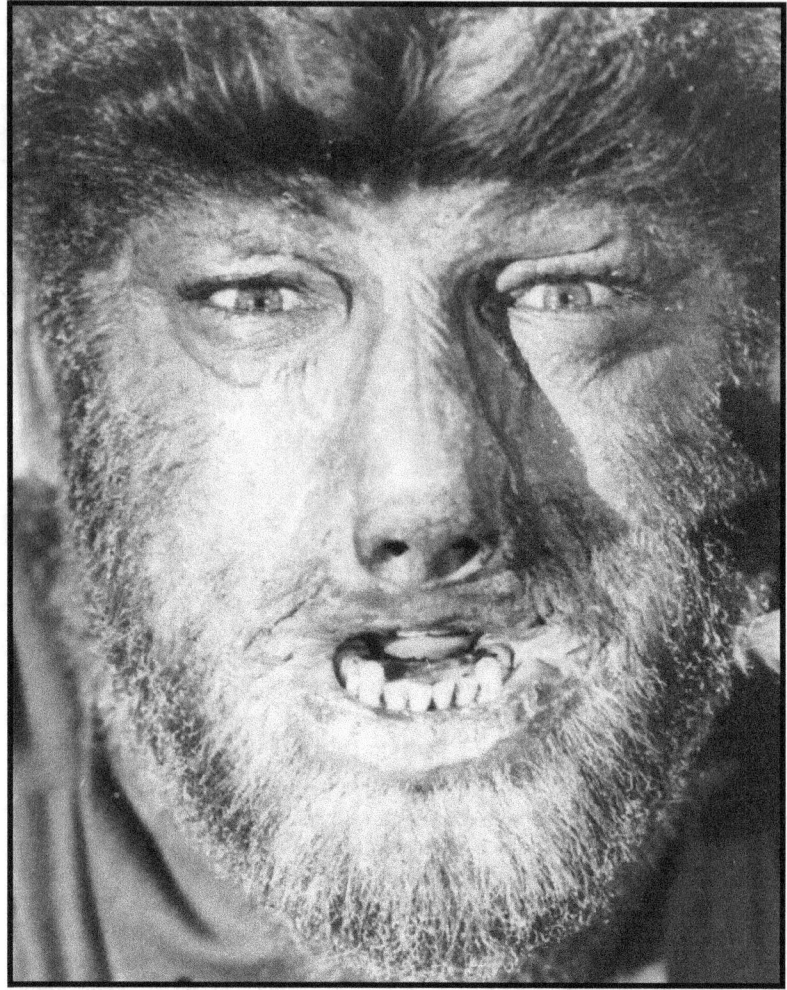

**Did *The Wolf Man* end the creative era of Universal filmmaking?**

in my opinion, it might be flowery, but it sure ain't poetry. In fact, I think one of the main criticisms of *The Wolf Man* is that for most of the movie (the sequences where Larry Talbot is a "wolf" in human form) the world depicted is a tad too literal and bland. But, Mark, I can see you love the movie, so let me step back and not challenge your subjective embrace.

**Mark:** I don't think many Universals from the 1940s are quite as polished-looking as *The Wolf Man*. Off the top of my head, I can't think of any of them that feature anything as impressive as the dry-ice forest from *The Wolf Man*—maybe the swamp from *Son of Dracula*.

**Arthur:** Well, I'm quite fond of *Frankenstein Meets the Wolf Man*'s graveyard and ice cave and the underground catacombs from *House of Dracula*.

**Mark:** Although you're right, Gary: There *is* a continuity of approach throughout the 1940s Universal horrors (how could there not be, since they often used the same artisans and sets?), but I think it comes together to better effect in *The Wolf Man* than in most other films. Also, I think that after 1942, there is a noticeable drop-off in production values—with the exception of bigger-budget specials like the 1943 *Phantom of the Opera*.

real—not the foggy, bare-treed "forest," not the gypsy carnival, not even the too-quaint village (obviously a back lot). All of which works in its favor, in an unlikely way. Everything looks too carefully calibrated, too *crafted*. In this aspect, *The Wolf Man* reminds me of the "poetic realism" of Marcel Carné pictures such as *Children of Paradise* (1945) and *Port of Shadows* (1938). Luchino Visconti's *White Nights* (1957) is another film that takes this approach: It was shot entirely on a set. Although the set is meticulously naturalistic, it nevertheless seems to be too perfect to be true, especially under Visconti's silvery, shadowy lighting. The result is that the film seems to take place in a dreamy Never-Neverland, but a Never-Neverland that seems eerily close by. Like you could take a wrong turn and stumble into it. In addition to its sets, *The Wolf Man*'s romantic fatalism also links it with those "high-brow" pictures I mentioned.

**Gary:** Mark, I do like your explanation of the poetry of *The Wolf Man*. Your comments about it being other-worldly are interesting, but I don't think such comments apply only to *The Wolf Man*. Look at other 1940s Universal horror movies, and I think you get the same world and same look. But,

**Gary:** To me *The Wolf Man* ended the creative era of Universal horror filmmaking and inspired *Frankenstein Meets the Wolf Man*, the first monster rally and the first juvenile-oriented B production, that left adult horror to the Val Lewton horror factory.

**Anthony:** By that token, couldn't one argue that *The Wolf Man* was the *last classic* Universal horror film?

**Mark:** I also feel compelled to point out that *The Wolf Man* has one of the greatest casts of any Universal horror film, and they acquit themselves nobly: Chaney gives the performance of his life; Maria Ouspenskaya creates one of the most memorable supporting performances in the entire Universal canon; Bela Lugosi has a hauntingly effective cameo; and the always-reliable Claude Rains and Evelyn Ankers come through as expected.

**Anthony:** Don't forget Warren William and Ralph Bellamy—and even Patric Knowles—also among the name cast and who deliver the goods.

**Mark:** Plus, it has a kick-ass werewolf! What's not to love?

**Gary:** Good points all, Mark. Good points all. Except for your point about *The Wolf Man* being Chaney's greatest performance. Sorry, but he's simply bad in the role. The performance of his life was Lennie in *Of Mice and Men* (1939). And I would make the case that *Son of Frankenstein* was the last classic Universal horror film. *The Wolf Man* was the forerunner of bland.

**Anthony:** I love Lon Chaney, Jr. in *Of Mice and Men*, but I think he's great in *The Wolf Man*, too. My feeling is that Chaney does well in a role that was a stretch for him. (Look—even though I love him, I'll admit it: *Many* roles were a stretch for him.) Except for one scene, when the bite on his chest has healed overnight and becomes a pentagram-shaped scar, and he has to tell his father, "Oh, but they're all treating me like I was crazy!" (or words to that effect). That line delivery strikes a false note. But otherwise he's just fine. (And that "treating me crazy" line is the one place where the scriptwriting stumbles. That scene ends abruptly, and the "crazy" line's almost a non-sequitur. I'll have to go back and watch it again, but the entire interchange doesn't play right. For that sequence, Siodmak must've rushed the pages out of his typewriter.)

Larry Talbot, coming on to Gwen Conliff, shows himself to be a figurative wolf that then becomes a literal wolf.

**Steven:** In my opinion, Chaney's performance as Larry Talbot is—not bad. There are moments when his emoting appears forced, such as when he breaks down and weeps in the crypt. And, at other times, Rains and Ouspenskya are clearly acting circles around him. But I think he handles the basic character arc smoothly enough. The key to this film is Chaney's metamorphosis from the happy-go-lucky American in the opening reel to a troubled and doomed character in the finale. Even given his missteps and limitations, Chaney still finds a way to pull it off. To my eyes, he has become a different character by film's end, which is the true test for any actor.

**Brian:** Which is why Chaney is more effective in *The Wolf Man* than he is in later entries in the series. He's playing a well-rounded character, someone who changes dramatically in the course of the film. I think Chaney does a great job with this—and I think this is a role that only Chaney, among the major horror actors of the time—could have played. Neither Karloff, Lugosi, Lorre or Price would have worked in the role. They couldn't have handled the "regular guy" aspect of the character. (Maybe Price, who wasn't so associated with horror roles at the time. But, still, has Price ever played a "regular guy"?) In the later films (starting with *Frankenstein Meets the Wolf Man*) Talbot and Chaney start to get annoying. The character becomes very one-note and whiny. Chaney isn't given a lot to work with, and ends up playing the role by rote..

The ice cave: Bela Lugosi as the Frankenstein Monster and Lon Chaney, Jr. from *Frankenstein Meets the Wolf Man*

**Mark:** Precisely. Talbot simply wallows in self-pity, moping around and bemoaning the fact that he can't simply die. It would be morbid if it weren't so dull.

I think Chaney is sensational in *The Wolf Man*, although the extent to which what he's doing can be considered a performance may be questionable. This is one of those fortunate instances where a role matches an actor perfectly: the suffering, in-over-his-head ne'er-do-well son who's trying to please his aloof and disapproving father, etc. Lon Chaney, Jr. simply *is* Larry Talbot. Even the fact that Chaney seems a bit out of his depth at points enriches the characterization, since Talbot's totally unequipped to deal with his situation. You look into Chaney's eyes and see that uncertainty and confusion, that unrequited yearning and anguish. It's very hard to discern the line where the character ends and the actor begins. Which, the way I see it, makes for a very impressive characterization.

**Anthony:** I avoided talking about *Frankenstein Meets the Wolf Man* because it has personal associations for me. But, so does *The Wolf Man*. *Frankenstein Meets the Wolf Man* was the first horror film I saw on *Shock Theatre*. I was 10. I sat through the moody, atmospheric opening that several of you have referred to, and all my 10-year-old brain was fixated on was seeing the Frankenstein monster. I had been hearing about the monster for a long time before I ever got to see a movie in which he appeared, and I couldn't wait. (On the other hand, nobody had ever told me stories about the lyncanthropic Larry Talbot.) For me, that whole first half-hour or so, leading up to the discovery of the monster in the ice, was only so much boring exposition that I had to endure before I got to the "good stuff."

A few months later, again on *Shock Theatre*, I got to see *The Wolf Man* for the first time—and the plight of Larry Talbot touched me in a way it hadn't when I was a callow youth, 90 days younger, watching *Frankenstein Meets the Wolf Man*. I felt guilty about not caring enough for Larry Talbot in the sequel after seeing him suffer in the original. Maybe that affected my attitude toward both films.

Certainly Roy William Neill was a much better director than George Waggner. Even so, *Frankenstein Meets the Wolf Man* is not a better film than *The Wolf Man*. Even if it had not been tampered with but had been released as it was filmed, with the monster's blindness and dialogue intact, I'm afraid that *Frankenstein Meets the Wolf Man* would not have reached the heights of *The Wolf Man*.

In those pre-video days, I never had the opportunity to purchase a print of *The Wolf Man*. However, I did receive, for Christmas, when I was 14, a reel-to-reel tape recorder from my parents. With this state-of-the-art machine, I recorded the soundtrack to many a movie—*Dracula* (1931), *Rio Bravo* (1959), *Marty* (1955), *All Through the Night* (1942)… and *The Wolf Man*. At a time when *Famous Monsters of Filmland* was just beginning its "filmbooks" (the first of which, as everyone probably remembers, was *Bride of Frankenstein*—in issue 21 [February 1963]), I had visions of breaking into print by doing a *Wolf Man* filmbook. In the summer of 1963, I lugged the tape recorder and the *Wolf Man* tape up to the cottage my family was renting for a two-week vacation, and, when everybody else was down at the lake, I was hitting "play" and "rewind," over and over, and transcribing the dialogue from the movie—my first step toward "filmbookization."

Needless to say, I never finished this project, which is why you never saw my name prominently displayed in the pages of *FM*. (Well, actually, I did get mentioned on the letters page of *FM* 25 [October 1963]—won a prize—for an epistle I wrote suggesting that *Kong* be remade in Cinerama, starring Karloff as Engelhorn, Price as Denham and Chaney and Carradine as the [albino] native chief and witch doctor, but that's another story.)

However, the exercise of listening to *The Wolf Man* and scribbling out the lines helped me immensely in catch-

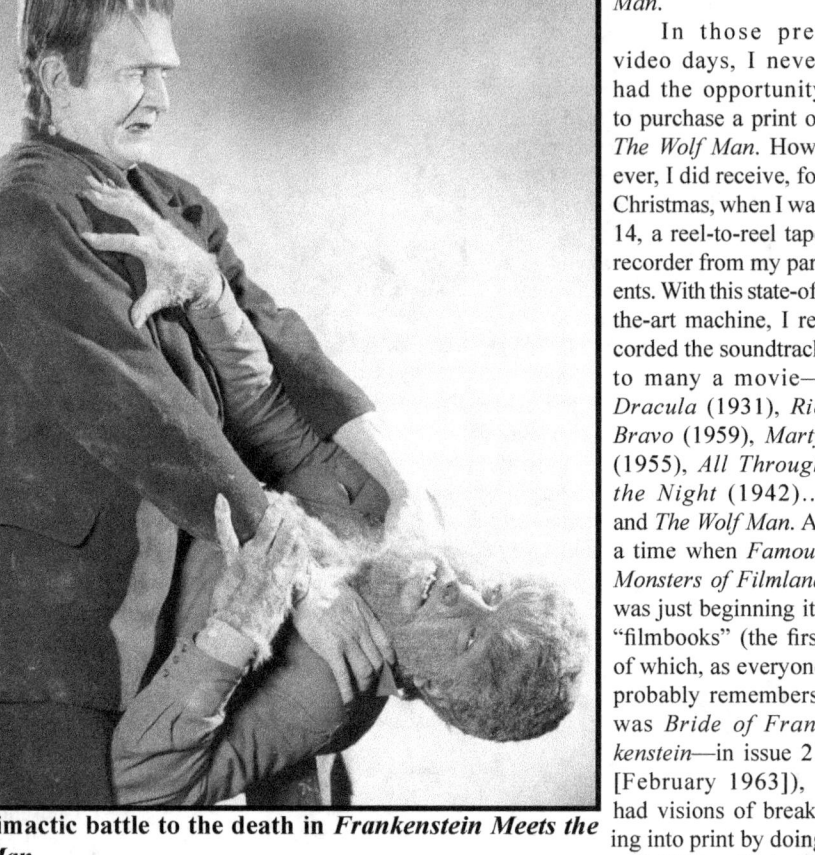

**The climactic battle to the death in *Frankenstein Meets the Wolf Man***

ing the many nuances in the film, and stood me in good stead when I came to write about it years later.

**Arthur:** We've all seen these movies too many times and had them wrapped up in so many of our memories that it is difficult to see them objectively.

**Anthony:** That's for sure. I will be the first to admit that warm and fuzzy memories do not a good movie make. A guilty pleasure maybe, but not a good movie. I have revisited *The Wolf Man* frequently since those heady days over 40 (*God!—40!*) years ago, and it has never lost its appeal for me—an appeal that Gary has (alas!) yet to find.

**Gary:** Hey, everyone: Driven by Anthony's comments, I really will watch *The Wolf Man* this weekend. I will be open-minded and see if I can get closer to the ideas expressed here recently. Most people seem to really like the film, so I owe it to myself to give it another shot.

**Steven:** Early impressions are hard to change, but you never know. I watched *The Mummy* a few weeks back and it affected me in a way that it never did before. The imagery of that movie really left an impact; it truly is a beautiful-looking film.

**Anthony:** We're standing on a precipice here: Gary vows to re-view *The Wolf Man* (due to our repeated endorsements of the film) and report on his reaction. The way he walks is thorny! (Hmm... that didn't come out quite right.) Here's hoping! I want to send him out with the words of Maleva ringing in his ears, but I can't remember the quote. (It's the incantation she gives Larry Talbot in the Gypsy camp, after she gives him the pentagram necklace. Joe Dante uses it as a coda to *The Howling* [1981]. "Go, now..." and I can't remember the more important part that follows!)—

**Steven:** "...And may heaven help you."

**Anthony:** Thanks, Steven. Well, let's hope he finds peace at last.

[*Time passes; Gary descends into his viewing room; everyone waits with bated breath...*]

**Gary:** Last night I re-watched *The Wolf Man* once again.

**Steven:** First of all, kudos to Gary for giving *The Wolf Man* another chance. And now, let the debate continue...

**Gary:** I will admit I enjoyed it *more* last night than I ever have, due to the fine pristine print provided by the Legacy presentation. I tried to enjoy the film's strengths, and there are several. First, the look of the actual production was impressive: the observatory, the antiques shop, the Talbot Castle interior, the Gypsy camp, the foggy marsh. Great art direction and set design. The film has a great look and sheen.

The second major achievement must go to Curt Siodmak—*not* for his script but for his wondrous werewolf mythology. The fortune-telling sequence at the Gypsy camp with Bela is wonderful. The creation of the "Even a Man Who's" poem is quite fitting, as are all the other lines of dialogue about a man bitten by a werewolf who survives becoming a werewolf himself. Every sequence with the Gypsy woman Maleva shines. Moody, creepy stuff, great horror myth making.

And of course we must mention the werewolf makeup and wolfish performance by Chaney wearing the yak hair. Iconic stuff. Superb.

But for me the movie ultimately disappoints for many, many reasons.

First of all, the thought of Rains' Sir John being Chaney's father is silly. Chaney is so hulking and Midwest America while petite Rains is a stuffy Brit. True, Larry lived in the States for 18 years, but the resemblance is just not there.

**Anthony:** A dialogue exchange between Sir John and Ralph Bellamy's Col. Montford addresses this dichotomy of height between father and son. Sir John claims that Larry takes after some Talbot ancestor with a name like "the Red Talbot" or something.

**Gary:** I am willing to bet that this "correction" was added to the script only after the casting was complete... a sloppy way to try to salvage the strange casting choices. Worse, when the family portrait shows that the dead brother looks just like Larry, one wonders what mom looked like!

**Anthony:** A low blow, Gary, picking on someone's mother!

Seriously, the resemblance between the brothers further indicates in what a shadow Larry lives—how his identity has already been compromised/questioned by the

Lou Costello and Lon Chaney, Jr. from *Abbott and Costello Meet Frankenstein*

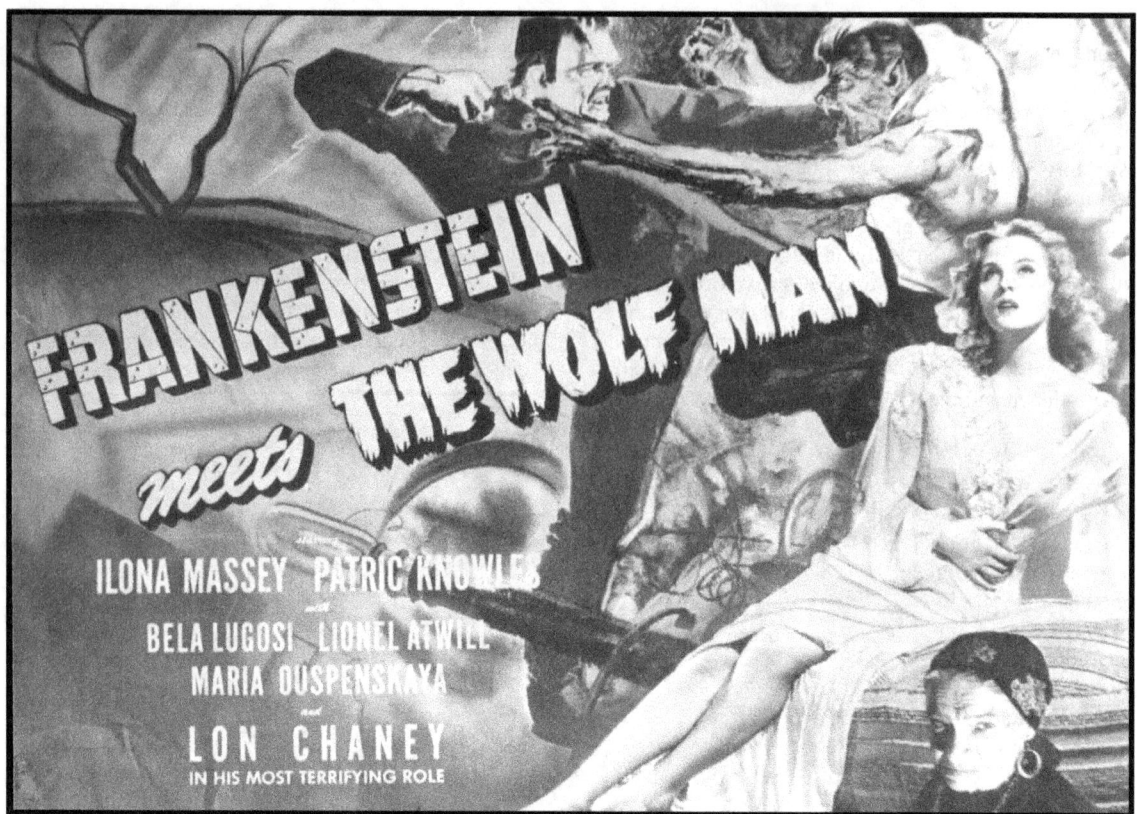

fact that dad always liked Larry's brother better. There's so much unspoken in *The Wolf Man*, which some may regard as a minus; here, I think, it allows for us to speculate like crazy about the marital difficulties of Sir John and [Lady?] Talbot. What prompted her to up and leave her husband *and ONE son* and take the other a continent away? Did Sir John mercilessly push his elder son the way we later see him pushing his younger? As I've said before: That infamous first "hunting accident"—just what was Sir John's responsibility for it? Now that the elder son is gone, a humbled-but-hiding-it Sir John has sent for his second son in a desperate attempt to ensure a Talbot heir.

**Gary:** Very thoughtful analysis here, Anthony. Some excellent points made. *But*, Chaney's performance is two-note. He either wears that dopey smile or wears that "the sky is falling" fearful face. Very little subtlety of performance exists... he either pushes the internal button for one or the other. The suggestion made here that Chaney was the only actor able to play the role is bogus. I am not saying that Karloff or Lugosi would have been the right choice, but some other pro out of left field (remember how Stanley Ridges was brought into *Black Friday* [1940] and stole the show from the horror vets?) could have demonstrated what a skilled *actor* may have created with such a juicy role. Chaney is passionate, and he tries very hard, but his limitations sink the performance. I will admit in wolf makeup he is superb. He makes a fine stunt man.

**Steven:** As I recall, the original point made was that Chaney was much better suited for the role of Larry Talbot than any of the other "name" horror actors. I don't think that point was bogus at all—I think it was spot-on. We can all speculate on whether Laurence Olivier would have made a better Wolf Man than Chaney (or a better Frankenstein than Karloff), but that's a different argument altogether.

**Gary:** First of all, Chaney, Jr. was a horror star in the making with only *Man Made Monster* (1941) in his fright résumé—

**Anthony:** Hey! Don't forget *One Million B. C.* (1940)!

**Gary:** —*ahem!*—As I was saying, Chaney, Jr. was a horror star in the making with only *Man Made Monster* in his fright résumé, so *The Wolf Man* was Universal's attempt to introduce a younger actor to step into the shoes of Karloff and Lugosi. Even so, Karloff, with the proper blend of pathos and ego, as evidenced by his wonderful performance in *The Invisible Ray* (1936), demonstrates what he could have brought to a portrayal of Lawrence Talbot. And it would have blown Chaney, Jr.'s performance out of the water. True, the younger romantic "wolf" would not have been right for Karloff in 1941, but it wasn't right for Chaney, Jr. either. Chaney botched the role; Universal would have been better served by casting some other actor to groom into a new Karloff or Lugosi. Karloff would have done a wonderful job as Talbot, if he were 20 years younger. If Universal got it right, the Universal horror factory may have survived longer than it did. Lon Chaney was a less-than-successful replacement for Karloff and Lugosi, and *The Wolf Man* illustrates this point.

**Anthony:** *Ahem!* I think it would have been great if Karloff and Lugosi had co-starred in the Henry Hull–Warner Oland roles in *Werewolf of London* (1935), and, while I find no fault with Claude Rains in *The Wolf Man*, I wouldn't have minded if Karloff had played Sir John, but I don't consider that a missed opportunity.

**Gary:** The movie is full of so many missed opportunities. Strangely, we see no full moon beaming and no human-to-wolf transformation following.

**Anthony:** That's because the rhyme says that a man may become a wolf "when the *autumn* moon is bright": the werewolf in this picture is a seasonal beast, not a menstrual one, as in the sequels. In fact, Gwen tells Larry that a werewolf is a man who becomes a wolf "at certain times of the *year*" (my emphasis).

You know, there are *two* criteria for becoming a werewolf, but I think that we and the filmmakers always forget the first one: "when the wolfbane blooms." I think the original intent was for the late-fall plant growth (an oblique homage to *Werewolf of London*'s night-blooming *mariphasa lumina lupina*?) combined with the harvest moon to effect the change—suggesting that, for three seasons of the year, when there was no wolfbane flowering, a victim was safe. When scriptwriter Siodmak switched it from autumn moon to full moon for *Frankenstein Meets the Wolf Man* (no doubt for the dramatic visual and so the stories wouldn't have to be limited to the fall all the time), he retained the "when the wolfbane blooms" part of the rhyme but essentially ignored it (since I doubt that wolfbane blooms in the winter, for example).

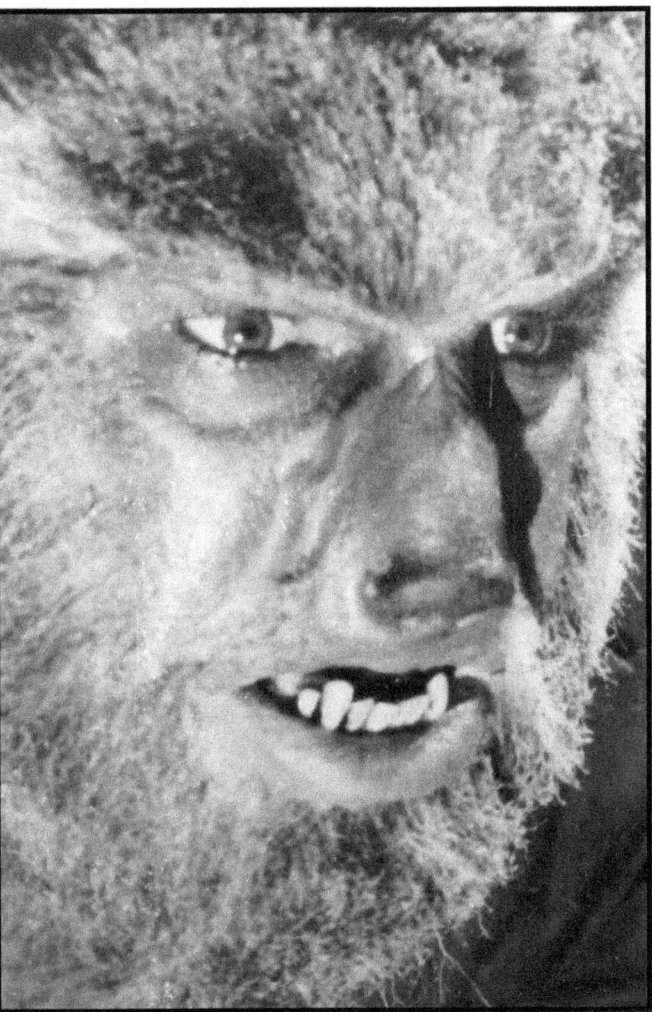

**Gary:** I don't buy this seasonal rationale. Larry was bitten by Bela and becomes a wolf seemingly during the next full moon—

**Anthony:** I think it's practically the *next night*, but I don't know if the moon is full or not.

**Gary:** So I don't see why the mythology could not have included a glowing full moon, no matter what the season!

And that "Even a man who… autumn moon is bright/ moon is full and bright" poem is repeated three times within five minutes and almost becomes silly. I almost expect a follow-the-bouncing-ball subtitle on the bottom of the screen. Spread it out; come on!

**Anthony:** We have to remember that audiences were hearing this folk wisdom for the first time in 1941, and the fact that the warning is repeated by different people merely indicates how wide-spread and well-known the folk belief is in the hamlet where Larry lives.

**Gary:** Three people repeating the mythic rhyme isn't my complaint—just the fact that it's recited by three people within five minutes.

**Anthony:** Well, actually, the poem is recited three times within *four* minutes, but who's counting? I don't think that's a flaw in a 70-minute picture that moves like gangbusters. At 9:52, Gwen introduces Larry the human wolf to the poem. At 11:30, Larry's rational father surprises him by repeating it (and logically arguing that it "has some basis in fact"—probably an "ancient explanation of the dual personality in all of us"). And, finally, at 13:45, on their way to the Gypsy camp, Jenny spies some wolfbane, which prompts her to reprise the verse. To the film's credit, Siodmak has Larry joke about it: "So you know that one, too?" Gwen's response seems to me fraught with meaning: "Of course. Everyone knows about werewolves."

**Gary:** To me, this is an error in the script, the editing and the film's pacing. Spread it out, and the same points are still made.

And the changes to wolf are noticeably undramatic. The first time Larry becomes a wolf follows a moody montage sequence of horrific images and a chat with his father before Larry is seen in his chambers, peeling off his socks to show hairy legs and feet. And then the legs transform, and we suddenly segue by dissolve to the marsh area with the same legs stalking, the camera pulling up to show the entire body. The marsh sequence is rather effective, but the hairy-legs sequence misses the mark.

**Chaney, Jr. lacks the acting chops to pull off such a nuanced performance.**

All the other sequences show Larry as the wolf suddenly appearing in the marsh, walking on tippy toes. Almost no kind of dramatic buildup is evident.

The script contains many such strange decisions, including the above and more. When the villagers are planting traps in the marsh, a minute later the Wolf Man is stalking the marsh and gets his leg caught... the sequence is slam-bam and seemingly rushed and without any exciting buildup. And, once Maleva comes upon the painfully wounded Larry, she tells the unconscious man to rest and find peace (with his foot and ankle severely damaged). And what is even more strange is having Larry, now in human form, barefoot and noticeably limping, get confronted by villagers who ask him what he's doing out here. And he answers he's hunting like the rest (barefoot in the woods without a weapon and limping?). The script cannot be forgiven for such odd choices.

**Anthony:** Your assertion that "the changes to wolf are noticeably undramatic" is much more damning than your objections to the Talbot father-and-son height differential or the repetition of the fatalistic folklore. I can only defend this by once again turning to the time in which the film came out and saying that—except for *Werewolf of London*—this was the first time lycanthropic transformations were shown onscreen. We'd have to compare their handling here to the earlier *Werewolf of London* or to March's 1931 *Dr. Jekyll and Mr. Hyde* to see how effective they are.

**Gary:** Okay, let's: *Werewolf of London* has a dramatic-transformation tracking shot *in 1935*, as the dapper Henry Hull passes by a series of columns, becoming progressively more wolfish as he does. And, of course, Fredric March as Hyde *in 1931* had a wonderful transformation. But now, five and 10 years later, *The Wolf Man* goes out of its way to be un-spectacular by showing quick cuts to a fully transformed werewolf and misses the opportunity to show an eerie man-to-wolf transformation.

**Anthony:** A friend of mine, some years ago, talked about the aptness and significance of Larry's legs and feet transforming. (This is something that Gary himself touches upon in his entry on *I Was a Teenage Werewolf* [1957] for *You're Next!*, Midnight Marquee Press's forthcoming book about loss of identity in horror films.) Back around 1984, my friend Leonard Heldreth delivered a paper at the Conference on the Fantastic about lycanthropy as a metaphor for puberty. He made the point that hair growth and changes in the feet are characteristic of adolescence/sexual awakening. So Larry (*I know; I know: he's* not *a teenager*) staring at his feet and seeing them change was appropriate.

**Gary:** A wonderful point here, and the reason why I love *Ginger Snaps* (2000), a fantastic film that develops this concept to the ultimate.

**Anthony:** I can't defend the "tippy toes" or pulling-up-of-pant-legs-while-prowling. I can only say that the film opts for an interesting approach to metamorphosis after the first transformation: The other two times when we see Larry changing, it's *from* a wolf to a human—when Maleva relieves him for an instant and when death reverts him to his former self. I think there's a thematic point being made here, but I'll leave its significance to others.

**Gary:** Bravo, again!

**Anthony:** I don't remember feeling that there was "no dramatic buildup" for the marsh scene where the wolf man gets his leg caught, but I'd have to watch the film again to see. Gary finds it odd that no one would wonder what Larry's doing barefoot and limping. But, with all that fog, how can anybody even *see* Larry's feet? And, with all that fog coming off the ground, wouldn't it be easy to stub one's toe? More importantly, whether the others know Larry's barefoot and limping or not, they would never in a million years assume that he was a werewolf, would they?

**Gary:** Very lame defense here, Anthony. Watch the film... the fog is not *that* thick, and his bare feet and limp make the sequence more than ridiculous; it is almost an embarrassment. Watch it again!

When Sir John ties Larry to the chair at the end (and even an old lady could get free of those straps), we never see the sequence where Larry becomes the wolf and struggles to free himself. Instead we cut directly to the full wolf in the marsh once again. And of course Siodmak has already telegraphed the ending by having the trussed-up

Larry demand that Sir John take his wolf's head silver cane before leaving. Again, the scripting is obvious, pedestrian and lacks drama.

**Anthony:** I never paid much attention to how tightly Sir John tied Larry to the chair. I don't know if it matters. (One could argue that Sir John tied him only half-heartedly for reasons or feelings of his own.) I never minded that we didn't see Larry-as-wolf tearing free from his bounds. (I would rather have seen Larry-as-wolf tear through his straitjacket with his teeth, as described in *Frankenstein Meets the Wolf Man*, but both achieve a certain effectiveness by being kept offscreen.) Rather than telegraphing the ending, Larry beseeching his father to take the cane is an example of foreshadowing.

**Gary:** Call it foreshadowing or telegraphing, but to me it is simply mediocre scripting.

Even the sequence when Jenny is killed is flawed. The obvious dog-as-wolf attacks Jenny to the right of the big tree (which prompts the question, "Why is Bela the werewolf an actual wolf and Larry, the Wolf Man, a man with wolfish features?"). When Larry enters the scene and the Bela wolf action moves to the left of the tree, we have a sequence as ridiculous as the one with Bela Lugosi in *Bride of the Monster* (1956), where Bela pretends to be fighting a giant octopus: Larry desperately holds a wolf doll to his neck and chest as he pretends to be fighting it off. The sequence is almost funny, and that's not good.

**Anthony:** Now, the problem of Bela-as-wolf being an actual wolf while Larry-as-wolf is a monstrous man—that is a problem. What can we say about it? Someone made a decision to hold back on the big makeup by using what looked like an animal in the first scene, thus retaining the surprise when we see the monster and, I guess, leaving some doubt in viewers' minds about whether Larry killed a wolf or a man. I don't know how to resolve this problem. It does make one wonder if there are two kinds of werewolves or something—those who go "all the way" and those who only half transform. Are we to think that, if Larry had lived with the werewolf curse longer, he, too, would eventually have become a four-footed beast during his transformations? (That certainly doesn't happen in any of the sequels.) No, I guess we just have to make do with what's onscreen as best we can. For me, the human-like monster that Larry becomes is scarier and more interesting than the plain old wolf that Bela becomes. I can see how, if the filmmakers had made both werewolves the same, they would have dissipated the scariness of Lon Chaney, Jr.'s makeup (either by showing something similar before we saw his—*or* by making him turn into an ordinary wolf).

**Gary:** A little Val Lewton would have saved the day here, right, Anthony? How about *not* showing the Bela wolf at all and just showing Talbot's reaction as he's beating the wolf? The cute little wolfie we see looks ridiculous and weakens the film. It would have been better to conceal and just suggest the creature.

**Anthony:** I guess my willing suspension of disbelief is better than yours—or I felt that the film's cuts covered up the phoniness—because I was always gripped by the attack on Jenny and didn't have trouble when Larry grappled with the wolf. (Comparing the fight to *Bride of the Monster*—now, that's nasty!)

**Gary:** Hey! I can suspend my disbelief as well as anyone else here, but the sequence where Chaney hugs the stuffed wolf is just as bad as *Bride of the Monster*'s octopus sequence. The beautiful pristine print only makes the wolf doll look sillier than ever.

And what could have been a pivotal theme in the movie is again botched terribly. Sir John (and even the film's opening scrolling text) makes the point that lycanthropy is a mental disease and that he believes his son suffers from mental illness. But all Larry can muster

**Chaney's performance is two-note. He either wears that dopey smile or wears that "the sky is falling" fearful face.**

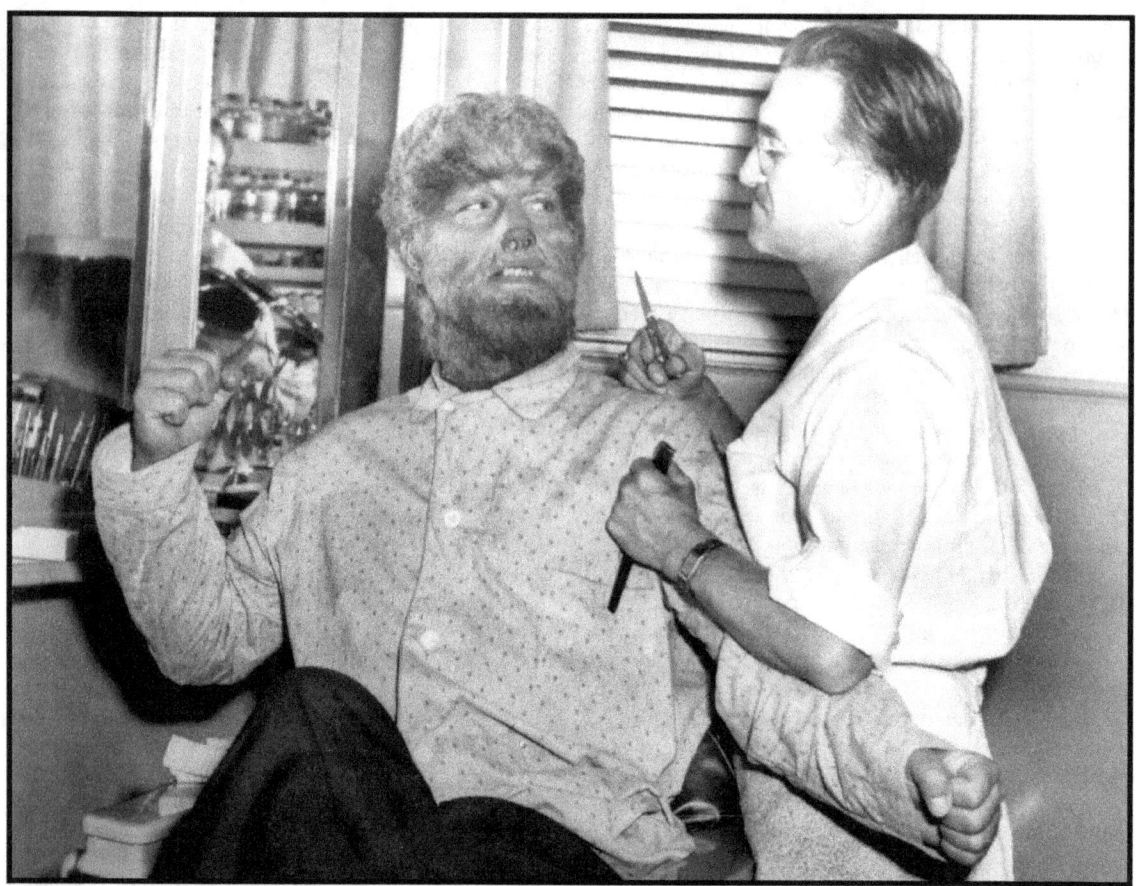

Jack Pierce applies the Wolf Man makeup to Chaney, Jr.

as counterargument is his famous "Give me tools and electronic devices—something that I understand—but don't ask me anything about theory" rant. Compare the psychological component in *Cat People* to the half-baked clunky concept created in *The Wolf Man*, and you'll see the difference between a theme artistically created vs. a poorly scripted one.

**Anthony:** If you prefer the "psychological" component in *Cat People*, Gary, there's not much I can say—except that *The Wolf Man* made *Cat People* and its "theme artistically created" possible. There are two different kinds of tragedy unspooling in these two films. Irena is a woman aware of her curse and struggling to overcome it. Larry is a man ignorant of what he's become and struggles to understand his changed status. Other writers here, wiser than I, have already spoken about the role of fate in *The Wolf Man*; I don't think fate plays as large a part in *Cat People*. *The Wolf Man* remains for me a tragedy of Aristotelian proportions, and I obviously admire the script more than you do.

**Gary:** My point is that the script is very flawed, and what could have been intelligent and dramatic seldom is. Of course, bland direction adds to the script woes.

My memory of *Cat People* tells me that the Serbian curse put on the tribe works hand in hand with destiny. And isn't it fate that a sexy young woman would eventually give in to her lustful feelings and turn into the panther? But, even if the dime-store psychology introduced in *The Wolf Man* were rethought as the sophisticated delivery of *Cat People*, I am willing to give credit where credit is due. However, the same logic can be applied to *The Wolf Man*, considering that *Werewolf of London* inspired this second werewolf film five years later. *The Wolf Man* is not an original but a rethinking of that earlier Universal movie.

**Anthony:** Thanks for keeping an open mind, Gary, and giving *The Wolf Man* another shot. I wish you could have liked it better, but I'm glad you found *some* merit in it this time around.

**Gary:** As stated, Anthony, you make some wonderful, well thought out points here, even though a few of your defenses are obviously stretches. But I think we can both move on here.

And, while I would never say *The Wolf Man* is boring, I would say the pacing is workmanlike and fails to generate the deterioration of Larry from wolfish, sex-obsessed predator to actual wolf predator. The script just doesn't offer the subtlety, nor does Chaney have the acting chops to pull off such a nuanced performance.

So *The Wolf Man* remains a movie of missed potential, featuring both poor and inspired acting and a few fantastic sequences that linger in the memory. The movie is more a concoction of individual sequences and marvelous sets and fog. But a classic Universal horror movie—*please!*

**Brian:** Gary, I enjoyed your detailed critique of *The Wolf Man*—you make a lot of good points about the film's flaws. But, truth be told, couldn't you do the same thing with virtually all of the classic Universal horror films? Certainly the direction in *Dracula* is less than inspired. *Frankenstein*, while brilliant in some spots, could be called pedestrian in others. The same is true of *The Mummy*.

These movies have such resonance for us is not because we saw them as kids, but because there's something primal about them. They're reaching into, or inventing, some kind of mythology that audiences respond to. As we get older and more discerning, we can tell the difference between a brilliant director like Whale and a hack like Browning. But, as much as we can admire the work of Whale and deplore the work of Browning, in one sense, the quality of the direction or the logic of the script is not really the point. *The Wolf Man* belongs up there in the pantheon with *Frankenstein*, *Dracula*, and *The Mummy* because it created a monster as memorable, and as seared into the public consciousness, as Frankenstein's Monster, Dracula, and the Mummy.

**Steven:** I would never place *The Wolf Man* on the level of cinematic high art. But I think that "well-executed craft" might be a fitting descriptor. And I, for one, think there is value in that. What's more, there is, in a very clumsy way, some magic to the film. Like Chaney himself, *The Wolf Man* rises above a pedestrian script and some noticeable talent limitations and creates something that has endured for over 60 years. Odds are, I think it will still be around long after modern imitators like *Ginger Snaps* (2000) and *Dog Soldiers* (2002) have crumbled to dust.

The Wolf Man in *House of Frankenstein*

**Gary:** I too like well-executed craft, and I love B productions and programmers. But the entire thrust of my argument was to show that the film's craft was flawed and lacking. I can name many other budget productions of the era that did a much better job with obvious limitations and rose above those limitations. Universal produced *The Wolf Man* with the intent of creating a new iconic monster to add to its canon, and, while the monster was classic, the movie itself is anything but. Yes, the film has endured for 60 years—merely because it introduced such a classic monster. The incredible monster and its mythology carried the movie on its back. It's a film that endured in spite of its quality! And whether or not *Ginger Snaps* endures as long is not our job but the job of time the revelator.

Perhaps too many people on these forums are shaped by their initial childhood impressions of this mediocre movie and need to revisit the film once again. We are no longer 10 years old!

I dedicate these rantings to Anthony Ambrogio, who inspired me to rethink my thoughts after giving the movie one more viewing.

**Anthony:** I humbly thank you. Of course, I wish you'd done a 180 after re-viewing *The Wolf Man*. The fitting, dramatic ending to this discussion would have been for you to write that, after seeing *The Wolf Man* again, you were totally blown away by it, saw the error of your ways and agreed with everybody else. But, *no*, you had to go and criticize the film in detail (while—I admit—giving it some credit).

**Bruce:** As I recently wrote Anthony, I've sort of gone full cycle on a lot of these films. I loved them as a kid, became overly critical when I took them (and myself) too seriously and now, in most but not all cases, I can watch them with affection and not too much scrutiny. (I no longer, for example, wonder how Larry Talbot, after turning into the Wolf Man while in his undershirt, must have rummaged in the closet and selected an appropriate shirt before going out into the night.) These movies are like old friends to me. Sorry if this is too simplistic.

**Gary:** If we get to the point where flawed icons like *The Wolf Man* are accepted into the same movie fraternity as *Frankenstein*, *Bride of Frankenstein*, *The Black Cat* (1934) and *Son of Frankenstein*—well, we might as well forfeit any credibility we possess as discriminating fans of cinema. We might as well get a keg of beer and applaud the body-count slasher movies and laugh hysterically every time a half-naked babe buys the farm. The fact that not all Universal or Hammer films are classics is what it's all about—creating a hierarchy where we dare say, "Now that's a really classic mythic monster, but too bad the film itself is so mediocre."

**Brian:** Well, first of all, I like watching half-naked babes buy the farm in slasher movies. But that's neither here nor there. I wasn't suggesting that all Universal horror movies are equal, or that they are exempt from criticism. What I'm saying is that what makes these films classics lies more in the mythology they created than in the quality of the filmmaking. Only a handful of the Universal horrors qualify as great films. In my view, *Frankenstein*, *Bride of Frankenstein*, *The Invisible Man* (1933), and *The Black Cat* would all deserve a spot on a list of the Top 100 Hollywood Movies Ever Made. In a hierarchy of Universal horror films, I would put *The Wolf Man* (and

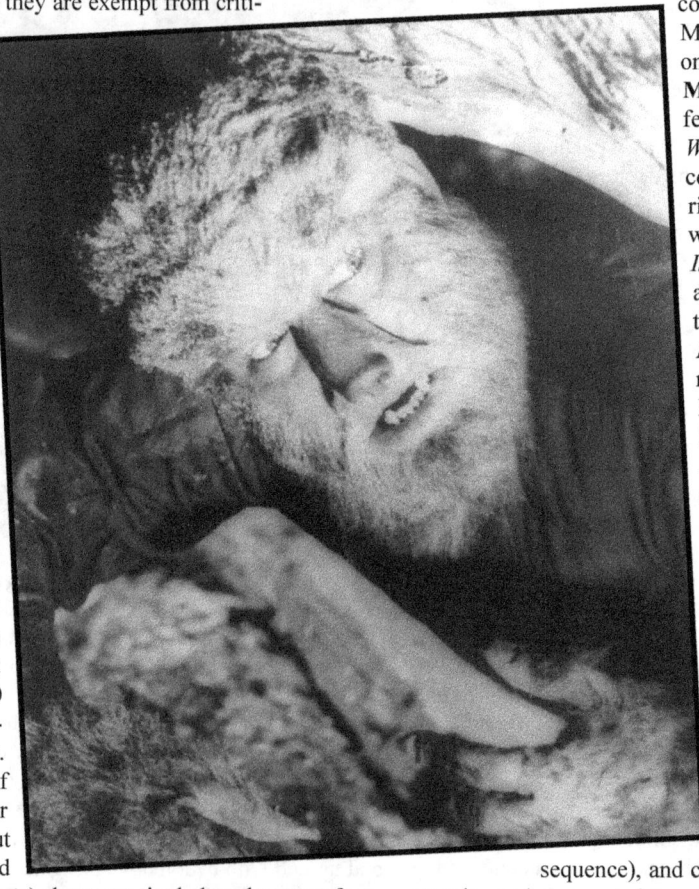

*Son of Frankenstein*) about one tier below those top four. Good, solid, entertaining films that created (or expanded on) a key mythology in the history of horror films.

**Steven:** Brian and I are completely in sync on this one.

**Brian:** Below those I would put *Dracula* and *The Mummy*—important movies, in places brilliant movies, but films with flaws deep enough to keep them out of the top two tiers. *Dracula* is ineptly directed; *The Mummy* is well directed but moves at a glacial pace. Still, the performances by Karloff and Lugosi (and Frye) in those films, and the iconographic nature of the monsters created in those films, put them firmly in the classics category.

**Gary:** Holding *The Wolf Man* above *The Mummy* is a crime to heaven of Cecil B. DeMillean proportions. Yes, *The Mummy* is very leisurely paced, but the reincarnation theme tossed side by side with a decaying reanimated 3700-year-old corpse lends itself to that type of pacing. *The Mummy*, besides being one of Karloff's greatest performances, features some of the best cinematography and direction in any Universal classic. Prof. Paul Jensen is correct here. *The Mummy* is a classic in every sense of the word. And, if people are putting *The Wolf Man* on a higher status, well, you can blow me over with a tana leaf! You can knock me down with wolfsbane. I just want people to say in a public forum that *The Wolf Man* is a better movie than *The Mummy*. I then want to print out copies and put them in personal files to be used to my advantage over the course of the next 20 years. My computer printer is turned on and ready.

**Mark:** For all my stated affection and respect for *The Wolf Man*, I must say that I consider *The Mummy* superior. In fact, I rank it—along with *King Kong* (1933), *Island of Lost Souls* (1933) and *The Black Cat*—among the top three or four Golden Age horror films *not* directed by James Whale. Personally, I revisit both *The Wolf Man* and *The Mummy* fairly frequently, and neither film has ever disappointed or bored me. But I must say I find the mystical/romantic sweep of *The Mummy* more consuming, Karloff's performance more mesmerizing than Chaney's. Plus, *The Mummy* opens with one of the scariest scenes of the Universal canon (the Bramwell Fletcher "He went for a little walk" sequence), and closes with one of the most stunning and unexpected moments of any Golden Age horror films (when the goddess strikes down Ardath Bey—a resolution that validates the existence of a non-Christian deity). *The Wolf Man* is still great, but *The Mummy* has this contest all wrapped up.

**Steven:** I would never say that *The Wolf Man* is a better film than *The Mummy*. By any intellectual standard, the latter is more polished, more artistic and more accomplished. But, as a viewer, I find *The Wolf Man* to be more accessible. I find myself returning to watch the plight of Larry Talbot far more often than I do the saga of Im-Ho-Tep.

**Brian:** But doesn't this mean that, despite *The Mummy*'s polish and artistry, you prefer *The Wolf Man* to *The Mummy*?

**Steven:** Absolutely. I respect and admire *The Mummy*. But, as a movie fan, I find *The Wolf Man* to be much more entertaining.

**Brian:** I was pretty shocked when I put *The Wolf Man* above *The Mummy* too. But the more I thought about it, the more it seemed to me that *The Wolf Man* is the better film. *The Mummy* is beautiful to look at; Karloff is great in it; the opening sequence is brilliant. I also like the flashback sequence showing the origin of the Mummy. The movie ranks very high in my estimation. But there are lots of dead spots in *The Mummy*. Long stretches of *The Mummy* are just boring to me. *The Wolf Man* never bores me. It grabs my attention from the first scene and keeps me engaged all the way to end.

**Gary:** Yes, *The Mummy* is slower paced, but to me the pacing is derived entirely from Karloff's slo-mo performance as Ardeth Bey! The director bases the pacing of the entire movie around the pacing of its chief character. Saying the movie is boring is missing the point... the pacing is part of its inner soul.

**Steven:** By that logic, the best horror films ever made were those safe and staid period pieces that MGM produced in the 1940s.

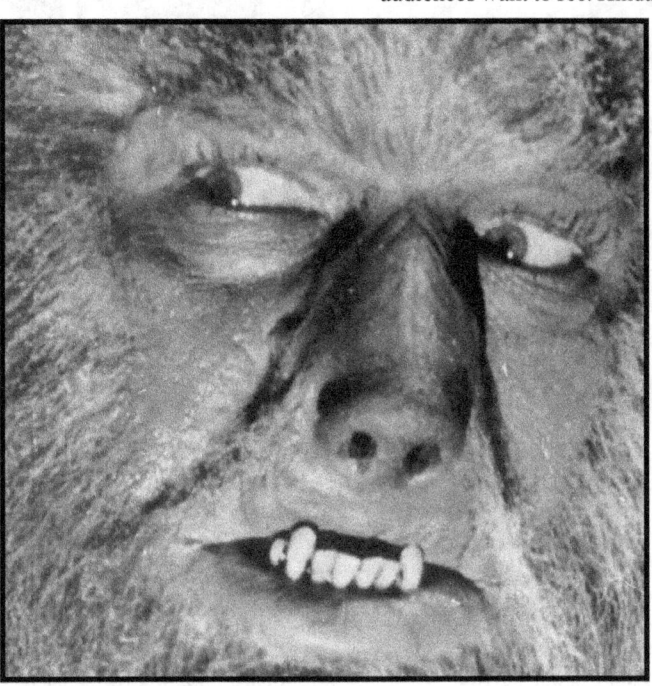

To me, the truly great movies balance artistic aspirations with the accessibility factor. A few good action scenes don't hurt either. *The Wolf Man* may err on the side of being a crowd-pleasing monster movie. But *The Mummy*, conversely, gets far too caught up in mood-lighting and deliberate pacing to be truly compelling cinema.

**Gary:** When I say "artistic," I am definitely not implying pretension or mainstream or big-budget production. Not all classics are slow paced; some are hyper-paced (like *Alien* [1979] and *Aliens* [1986], which are true horror-film classics). But some classics take their time and move at their own rhythms. *The Mummy* is one of those films. Its creepiness, in part, comes from its pacing. To me, it is compelling cinema, and its mood and pacing make it so. But that doesn't mean that all horror classics are slow. *Bride of Frankenstein* is not slow, but it is definitely a challenging movie experience with its quirky performances and abrupt changes in tone. Sometimes we have to drop our expectations and accept a film at face value. How many people actually put down *Cat People* because we never saw Simon Simone transforming into a cat/panther? The point is, Steven, unlike what you suggest, classics do not compromise for their audience. That's why David Lynch movies such as *Blue Velvet* (1986) and *Mulholland Dr.* (2001) are such gripping, intense and disturbing cinema classics. The audience is asked to drop all its preconceptions and accept the film for what it is artistically. All great films do this, and, as soon as you say classic films must be accessible, you miss the point. Great art demands that the reader or viewer rise up to its level to reap the inherent rewards. Accessibility amounts to pandering to an audience and reshaping the product to the preconceived idea of what audiences want to see. Kinda like selling cereal. What applies to Rice Krispies does not apply to the cinema of Whale, Wise, Lynch, Welles, Fisher or Zombie. Classic films always challenge the viewer. We must rise up to them; they definitely should not lower the bar downward to us.

Classics are never "staid" and "safe." They challenge us and present things in new ways.

**Anthony:** I don't mind working to figure out a story, but, if there is no level of accessibility—no way into the art; nothing to make a reader/viewer care about it—why bother to look further? For me, Shakespeare is the epitome of what an artist should be: He tells stories that anyone can enjoy. But he has levels upon levels that allow discerning and interested readers and auditors to delve deeper and deeper. And I will admit in a public forum that *The Wolf Man* is a better film than *The Mummy*.

This is not to say that *The Mummy* is crummy. I wrote, just recently, I think, that my feelings about *The Mummy* fluctuate from viewing to viewing; one time I think it's the cat's pajamas (that's Bast, the cat god) and then next I think it's the slowest thing since molasses. The fact that it's essentially *Dracula* with sand sometimes works to its disadvantage; other times I'm fascinated by its atmosphere.

But, as is painfully obvious by now, I love *The Wolf Man*. For me, it moves quickly and inexorably to its "predestined end." I admire its strengths and overlook its (few) flaws.

What can I say?

Well, okay, now I've said it. Gary has my statement in his files and can use it for whatever nefarious purpose he has in mind!

# Universal's Crown Prince...
## Evelyn Moriarty Remembers Carl Laemmle, Jr.
### by Gregory Mank

When the end finally came September 24, 1979, it seemed a bitter, mocking joke.

For years, the small, wizened old man had been seriously ill. All his life he'd been a severe hypochondriac, but by 1979 he was a very sick man—crippled, reduced, described by some as living the life of a vegetable. When death truly approached, he lay in his bed in the house on Tower Grove Drive, high above Beverly Hills.

In the living room, on a bookshelf, his 1930 Academy Award—nearly a half-century old—vigilantly kept a deathwatch.

Even then, at age 71 and seeming much older, he was still called "Junior." Once upon a time, from 1929 to 1936, Carl Laemmle, Jr. was the "Crown Prince" of Universal City, California. He'd personally produced *All Quiet on the Western Front*, still the most honored film in the 90-plus year history of Universal Studios. *Back Street* (1932), *Imitation of Life* (1934) and *Show Boat* (1936) were all Carl Laemmle, Jr. productions. And Junior had launched the 1931 horrors *Dracula* and *Frankenstein,* creating a genre that became American folklore, still pumping blood into Universal's sprawling worldwide empire of 2006.

Yet, by the time of his death and for many years previous, "Junior" Laemmle was a Hollywood ghost. He hadn't produced a film in over 40 years. Even in his prime, as Universal's "Baby Mogul," Hollywood-at-large unfairly regarded him as a joke. Junior was a symbol of the rampant nepotism that had compromised the legend of his father, Universal founder Carl Laemmle—who'd given Junior the post of Universal's General Manager April 28, 1929 as a 21st birthday present. Tyrannical father and his neurotic son fought bitterly. Junior found his job no compensation for his father's wrathful vow of disinheritance if Junior had married actress Constance Cummings, whose loss Junior considered the tragedy of his life. Ironically, only a few months before Junior's death, Ms. Cummings, after decades of personal and professional joys, won Broadway's Tony Award (at age 69) for her triumphant performance in the play *Wings*.

Evelyn Moriarty, Junior's lady friend since the early 1940s, was still, as she called herself, his "Saturday night date." The former Earl Carroll beauty and Marilyn Monroe stand-in visited Junior, a faithful friend all those years to a man who—while she was on location in *The Misfits*—had babysat her poodles and had written her letters from them. They watched TV in his bedroom, and she tucked him in at night, the sheet so tight against him that, as Evelyn recalls, Junior "looked like *The Mummy*," the Universal horror classic of 1932. Evelyn was concerned about Junior, the eccentricities of his late life and the German female housekeeper who, come the night, locked Junior in his room.

"It was like something out of *Sunset Boulevard*!" says Evelyn Moriarty of Laemmle's final days and nights.

Did Count Dracula, Frankenstein's Monster, The Mummy, The Invisible Man or the Bride of Frankenstein ever caper in Junior's nightmares? Probably not. Evelyn Moriarty rarely heard Junior talk of those old films, and the few historians who met him found him with little to say. His father's memory always lingered oppressively, whose shadow Junior never escaped and whose tyranny Junior couldn't forgive. One might argue that receiving the studio at age 21, producing classic movies, was the worst thing that ever happened to Junior Laemmle —considering the personal price he paid for it.

And when Death finally arrived at 1641 Tower Grove Drive, late in the afternoon of September 24, 1979, it paid its call on precisely the 40th anniversary of Carl Laemmle Sr.'s death.

The funeral was pitiful.

The venerable Rabbi Magnin, who officiated at Laemmle, Sr.'s funeral in 1939, noted Junior's sad final existence, saying the Junior the mourners had known and loved had gone on before Carl Laemmle, Jr. was buried with his father in the Chapel Mausoleum at Home of Peace Cemetery in East Los Angeles.

Yet, in the wake of Junior's death, another sad indignity occurred.

Junior's Academy Award disappeared.

Evelyn Moriarty in her costumed dancing days.

**Many dramatic and conflicting stories circulate about the personality and the talent of Junior Laemmle. You knew him for over 40 years?**

Yes. He was very sweet. He was very good.

**Before we discuss Junior, please give me a little background about yourself, and how you came to Hollywood.**

I came here with *George White's Scandals*. I was underage!

**And how did you become an Earl Carroll showgirl?**

I needed a job and I didn't know how to do anything! I was about the right height and type in those days. Earl Carroll's was near Sunset and Vine, a little up from Vine. It later was the Aquarius, and Ed McMahon had his talent show there. I think that was the happiest time of my life... everybody went in there every night of the week.

**They say you knew everyone. There's a clipping that stated you were called in as a witness in the Lionel Atwill orgy trial.**

What it was... somebody asked me if I wanted to go swimming, out in Malibu, one day, one Sunday, a weekend, and we went out to this beach house, and I really went swimming. It was cold, it was when I first came here, and I'd only been here a short time... around 1940. It was kind of a nasty, dreary day in May or June. Then we went out and got something to eat, and the next thing I know, about six months later, I'm subpoenaed to the Grand Jury, with Lionel Atwill!

Well, I was only a kid! I wasn't 16 years old, and it scared the hell out of me! I was afraid I'd be put in jail! I took a cab *(laughing)*, and I went up to his room and I said, "Will you please pay the cab bill?" It seems he was supposed to have shown stag pictures or something like that—well, to this day, I've never seen stag pictures, I have no use for them, and I didn't see any. I was actually out in the water, swimming. I do remember there was something in the paper... "What Earl Carroll Beauty Went to the Grand Jury and Demanded to Have Her Taxi Cab Paid?"

**Evelyn Moriarty in closeup**

Anyway, I said to the Grand Jury, "No, I didn't see any stag pictures, I was swimming," and I added, "If they *did* show pictures I wouldn't have seen them anyway, because I can't see—I'm very nearsighted and I didn't have my glasses!" (*laughing*) And they just looked at me and laughed and let me go! The whole thing was crazy.

**As for Junior Laemmle...did you meet him at Earl Carroll's?**

No... I came out here in *George White's Scandals* and we were working at the Biltmore. As I told you I was underage and could have gotten into a lot of trouble, but I didn't know any better, and everybody was very nice to me. Around that time Harry Ritz, of the Ritz Brothers, told me that Hollywood would groom me and if I got in any trouble he'd give me the money to go back home, to New York, Long Island, where I belonged. So I was sort of protected.

Anyhow, I met Junior. I was doing *Scandals*, I was only here a couple of days, and some publicity men took me to a nightclub called *The Little Troc*. I did not know one name in Hollywood, I didn't know what a producer was and I didn't know what a director was—*very* uneducated. The Ritz Brothers were there, I was dancing with Harry Ritz, and this little guy with this big smile is sitting there with the governor's son. They stop at the table and they introduce me to Carl Laemmle, Jr. I couldn't *pronounce* his name let alone *remember* it! They said that he was a producer. I didn't know enough to play up to him because he was a producer; I just went on my merry way. Anyway, the governor's son came over to our table, and I said, "Well I met the *President's* son"—Roosevelt Jr.—I met him one day backstage in New York.

Anyhow, I was invited up to his house to go swimming. (Oh, swimming—ha! Ha!—when I say swimming, I think of that Lionel Atwill thing!) And the next day the publicity man picked me up and drove me up to 1275 Benedict Canyon, next door to where Harold Lloyd lived. We went up this private driveway, and up to this big place—and I thought Junior was sort of like the *manager* of this place! And they got a kick out of me, because I was unaffected! So that's how I met him.

**What struck you about him right away?**

Nothing very much! But this big estate, I thought that he was the manager or something—I didn't think he *owned* the big estate!

**So he didn't take umbrage, and didn't feel a big need to impress you?**

I don't think he had to go out of his way to impress anybody—everybody was out to get what he or she could from him.

**So this was around 1940, and he had left Universal...**

And MGM. He was about 32, and already retired!

**And he was living on the old Laemmle estate in Benedict Canyon?**

Yes. They later sold the place, in the 1950s I think, when a million dollars was a lot of money. They sold it, tore down the original house, sold the glass that had silver in it, and the beams, and subdivided the property. So while he was waiting for a house to be built on the top of Tower Grove Drive, above Beverly Hills, he lived in one of George Cukor's houses, on Cordell Drive. Cukor had three houses built on his property. Spencer Tracy had one of the houses, and a man who was the head of an automobile company had another one, and Junior had the third one—he rented it.

**What about his personality?**

Well, I think he was shy... I just remember that I used to call him "Poor Little Rich Boy." I felt sorry for him.

Even though I told you I was uneducated, and didn't know, I did know that all these people were out to clip him. The trouble with Junior was that he was too honest... And another thing about him was that he was used to having complete control. When they sold the studio, he went over to MGM, and he had to do what somebody told him to do. He couldn't take it. He had very good ideas, but you know how people are, people with ideas—other people try to pull them down and don't want them to do well.

**Did he realize people were out to "clip" him?**

Yes and no. He only put out so much, they could only get so much, and that was it.

**Were you ever officially engaged to him?**

No.

**But you were friends all the rest of those years?**

Uh-huh.

**What was he doing in his retirement? Hobbies?**

He went to the racetrack. He was a big gambler.

**Was he much for nightlife?**

He was before he got sick. He went to a lot of theaters and a lot of movies. And places to eat, like Perrino's. He didn't like nightclubs so much, because he didn't like the air-conditioning. He would have it turned off!

**You mentioned he got sick. Various reports claim he was sick the last 10 years of his life.**

*Twenty* years.

**His hypochondria was supposedly legendary.**

Yes, he was known as hypochondriac. I think his father was too—I read that his father was. And he would always be with the doctor. If someone coughed in the room with him, he would go check out the doctor, he wouldn't let anybody with a cold around him. He thought he had sinus trouble, wouldn't have flowers... In the beginning, when this first happened to him, he had some friends who were dying of heart attacks, so he started walking kind of funny—I went through this thing with him—instead of bending his legs when walking, he'd walk with his legs real stiff—like a goosestep. Well, what happened was, he used to fall. He went into a hospital, had a check-up, came home, got a private nurse—and for 20 years, he was in bed.

Eveyln Moriarty looks gorgeous in her show costume holding a bouquet.

**He was living on Tower Grove by this time?**

Mm-hmm. He should have never moved out of Benedict Canyon, because there he had to walk down the steps! (*laughing*)The Tower Grove house was one-story.

**What kept you close during all those years?**

Well, you see, Greg, I came from the other side of the tracks. I didn't know how to eat; I didn't know anything. Junior was very good—Junior *watched me grow up*. Junior was very good to me. He was always there if I needed anything. He bought me a dog when I got a divorce—he

Director James Whale and Ernest Thesiger on the set of Junior Laemmle's greatest artistic triumph, *Bride of Frankenstein*

was a very good friend. And I had these little poodles, and he used to babysit them! I once had a family of poodles, and after they all died—this was the last present he ever gave me—Junior got me a little Shitzu that I just buried last week. He said, "You have to have a dog, you have to have a little dog!" I think it was because he knew damn well I'd stay home and take care of the dog instead of going out! And he used to like to see her, I'd take her up there, and he used to throw food at her! And I used to tell him, that if he didn't stop, I was never going to bring her up there again, because with these dogs, he used to buy them filet mignon!

You know, I was connected with Marilyn Monroe. And people are always asking me about Marilyn—she was the most wonderful girl who ever lived. When I went to Reno to do *The Misfits* (1961), my dogs used to stay up at Junior's house. And he wrote me *letters* from the *dogs*! The *poodles*! So Junior was very sweet. He was just *good*.

By the way, Junior wanted to produce *Rain* with Marilyn. He wanted to do things—people were always after him for something, but then when he wanted to acquire a project for himself and needed distribution or stuff, nobody wanted to help him.

**So he was a true friend to you.**
Yes he was. I remember one time when I first was around, and Mervyn LeRoy saw me at the racetracks, doing some charity work for Warner Bros., and he came into Earl Carroll's and said he was going to make a star out of me. He sent the car from MGM to come get me, and I go to his office, and I told Junior everything. So Junior called Leroy and said, "You leave her alone, she's a good girl!" He protected me.

**Do you think with different doctors Junior might have rallied?**
Oh, he was waiting for Dr. Salk to find a new vaccine for him. And these doctors would come, but what they did, they *yessed* him to death, and he wasn't doing anything to help himself. Like he didn't try to walk. He said, "I can't walk, I can't walk." And I remember one doctor saying, "If you don't use your muscles, then they're going to deteriorate, other things are going to get bad with you." And that's something he wouldn't do. When he first got sick, he'd go to this clinic—in those days $25 was a lot of money—this clinic at Cedars, it was Cedars of Lebanon then, and they used to put him in the pool. He'd get mad at this doctor because he wanted somebody to pick him *out* of the pool—he didn't try to get out himself. So he stopped going. He wouldn't *try*. He was waiting for a miracle drug. He would send himself flowers—even though he thought flowers made him sick! He was almost like Howard Hughes! It was a real strange situation, now that you made me think of it!

**Did he ever express interest in resuming his career?**
Yes. At one point he had the option on the book *Butterfield 8*, the movie for which Elizabeth Taylor won an Oscar. About the time of *Bonnie and Clyde* (1967), maybe before it, he'd written a letter to Jack Warner and thought they ought to put their two heads together and make *The Son of Rico* or something.

**"Rico" was the character Edward G. Robinson played in Warner Bros.' *Little Caesar* (1930).**
Junior loved gangster pictures! And then toward the end, he hired the man who wrote *The Fly* to come over and they were writing a play, *The Invisible Woman*, because Junior had done the film *The Invisible Man*. But it didn't go anyplace.

**How was his mental state in his final years?**
He was clear, but he lost interest in a lot of things. I used to—and it was almost like a job with me—I used to go up there to Tower Grove, and I was like his Saturday night date. And he'd come to the table, and then he would go back into his bedroom and go to sleep. He would lose

interest. The way people could keep his interest was to talk about the older times. Now a lot of people who had worked for him at Universal, they used to talk about the different things that happened.

**And he enjoyed that?**

Yeah. Lew Ayres, from *All Quiet on the Western Front*, used to come up at the end. And Lewis Milestone, who directed the picture—Junior called him "Millie." And Paul Kohner, but he was another phony. And John Huston. Junior gave John Huston his first job. Walter Huston came to Junior and said, "John needed a job," and Junior said, "Okay, he starts tomorrow." Junior was a very *kind* man. But Junior… he lost confidence in people. He once told me that, in the old days, he couldn't get up in the morning and pee without Mervyn LeRoy calling, but after he didn't have a studio, Mervyn LeRoy didn't talk to him! Jean Renoir was one of his best friends until he died (and he didn't meet him at Universal). What a darling little man he was, and a very *simple* man.

**Did Junior ever reminisce with you about his Universal years?**

No. But when he used to lie in bed, I used to tell him he was just like *The Mummy* in his picture! He used to put the covers right up to his neck and tuck them in, beneath the sheets! I don't know how he moved in that bed!

You see, I wasn't there to clip Junior or anything. I was *real*. I didn't "yes" him. If I thought something was wrong, I'd say something was wrong. I'd see somebody and I'd say to Junior, "Ah, he's a phony."

**I imagine this won you a lot of trouble from the people out to clip him!**

Well, with a lot of the people, I was an outsider. I was "the showgirl," I was "the gold digger." But believe me, I gave more to Junior than he gave to me! (*laughing*)

**At the end, Junior had a housekeeper, who was really a German housekeeper… Are you Jewish?**

No.

I used to tell Junior that, with his housekeeper, that was another case of a German killing a Jew! She thought she owned the house! And you know these old German people, or European people, the men come first. They sit at the table and all that…

Oh golly, the whole thing was weird!

**So she dominated?**

More or less. When she first moved up to the house she had a room in the back, the maid's room, then she moved up front, and finally she decided to lock him in his room. And I said, "What if you have a heart attack?" She'd lock him in his room and sit on the couch near his door. And then she used to tell awful stories about me. When I say tell awful stories, I was the outsider, but if I stayed away, he called. He had his television in his room, and he used to watch television there. And I used to sit there and watch television too. That's all I was doing, believe me. And she went around telling some strange stories… I told her if she didn't shut up, I was going to tell him what I'd heard.

**She intimated things of a lewd nature?**

Yes, yes yes. That's right… before she came, his bedroom was like everybody's living room, and he entertained in his bedroom. People would come up and he'd talk to you, he didn't feel like getting up. He'd be in bed. That was his way.

**Why would she lock him in his room?**

I do not know! …The whole thing was bizarre, believe me! I used to tell people, "It's like *Sunset Boulevard*!"

**What can you tell me about his death and funeral?**

It was disgraceful.

I hadn't gone up the weekend before, because I was told he was sick and didn't want to see anybody. He'd had a stroke, and he was pretty sick. His niece Carol, his

**Boris Karloff and James Whale on the Universal studio set**

sister's daughter, had moved up to the house, to watch things. When he died, she called me.

I didn't see the body, because I was working. I attended the funeral. But I understand he was buried in a T-shirt that I had bought him. I used to go out and buy him cotton T-shirts because, in the end, the last few years of his life, he didn't wear shirts. He was a terrific dresser at one time, but they used to just put these T-shirts on him. So I used to go out and buy him these pretty blue ones and yellow ones, colored ones, to give him more color. And I understand that he was buried in a T-shirt, and a scarf wrapped around his neck!

**Why?!**

I don't know. I don't know.

**What precisely happened at the funeral?**

Rabbi Magnin officiated at it. There was a very small crowd. Carol gathered all of the flowers that were there and took them home in the limousine.

**I believe Rabbi Magnin had spoken at Laemmle, Sr.'s funeral. Did he speak well of Junior?**

Oh yeah, but as Rabbi Magnin said, the Junior that they knew wasn't there anymore, he had gone before. And Rabbi Magnin was one of his trustees or something, and at the end, Rabbi Magnin didn't want any part of it. There was too much fighting going on.

**Where was Junior buried?**

It was out at the Home of Peace, that cemetery where his father is… in East Los Angeles… It's a Jewish cemetery.

**What happened to the Academy Award he'd won for *All Quiet on the Western Front*?**

It disappeared! I don't know whether the Oscar disappeared while he was still alive, around the time he died or whether it disappeared later… but they couldn't find his Oscar. It used to be over with the books. A lot of times I'd pick it up.

That's the way it was. He always had people around, and they ignored everybody there but played up to him, to see what they could get out of him. I used to go there one week and I'd see something, and the next week it would disappear!

**You mentioned fighting about his estate. Was there much left?**

He didn't have very much. Some paintings. There was a lien on the house. If he hadn't died, he might have ended up being homeless, or at the Motion Picture Relief.

**It seems he deserved a lot more than he got.**

Everybody here gets hurt.

Yes, Junior was good. If something was wrong at the studio and I was unhappy, he knew it. I wouldn't have to say anything to him. And he would always ask, "Was it a Jewish person or a Christian?" If it were a Jewish person, he'd buy me a present! And if it were a Christian person, he'd buy me a present! It didn't matter who did it, he always did something to make up for what somebody did. Really!

**So he was always there for you.**

Yes he was.

As for the missing Academy Award…at one point, in 1995, the Oscar and Junior's personal script for *All Quiet on the Western Front* were on the auction block at Butterfield and Butterfield. A spokesman there was unable to give me any information as to whether or not the sale ever took place.

Carla Laemmle, Laemmle, Sr.'s niece, naturally hopes to find the long-missing Oscar and donate it to the Laemmle Museum in Laupheim. If anyone has any information, please contact me c/o *Midnight Marquee*. Thank you!

# THE THREE FACES OF UNIVERSAL'S DRACULA

### BY BRIAN SMITH

Dracula is the most controversial of Universal's classic monsters. Everyone agrees that the Wolf Man is always the Wolf Man. He doesn't change much from film to film. Everyone agrees that the Frankenstein Monster is always the Frankenstein Monster. He does change over the course of the series, but his metamorphosis from intelligent if childlike creature to brain-dead hulk can be attributed to such things as botched brain transplants, prolonged comas and extremely traumatic first dates. But Dracula's personality and character traits change from film to film without even an implied explanation. This, and the gaping holes in Dracula's continuity (contrasted with the relatively tight continuity for the Wolf Man and the Monster), leads to one inevitable question… how many different Draculas are there, anyway?

The obvious answer is one. But there's another possibility. It could be that the Universal Dracula films are not about one vampire named Count Dracula. Rather, they're about three distinct vampires: The real Count Dracula, who appears in *Dracula* and (as a corpse) in *Dracula's Daughter,* and two imposter vampires who call themselves Count Dracula. These two imposters also go by the names Count Alucard (*Son of Dracula*) and Baron Latos (*House of Frankenstein* and *House of Dracula*).

Unlike its Frankenstein and Wolf Man films, Universal's Dracula films rarely provide an explanation for Dracula's return. Dracula is destroyed at the end of one film and mysteriously, reappears in the next. Each Universal Dracula film asks us to accept the fact that its Dracula is *the* Dracula. But we have only Universal's word for it that this is the same Dracula that we saw in the previous film.

If the Universal Dracula films are all independent, stand-alone movies, then all three vampires are Count Dracula. They are merely different interpretations of the same character. But, if the Universal Dracula movies are to be considered a series, then the Draculas in the later films cannot be the same Dracula who appears in the first film. Their behavior, their manner, their skillfulness as vampires are too radically divergent. The most plausible explanation for this divergence is that these are three separate and distinct vampires with little in common except a penchant for formal attire.

### COUNT DRACULA
*Dracula* (1931)
*Dracula's Daughter* (1935)

The true Dracula, of course, is the original Count as depicted in *Dracula*. This Dracula (Bela Lugosi) is a charming fellow. When he first meets Renfield (Dwight Frye), and later the Sewards (Helen Chandler and Herbert Bunston), he is all smiles and courtliness. He is every bit the aristocratic, well-bred gentleman. Despite this outward appearance of normality, there's something about him that's unsettling. The shooting script for *Dracula* describes Renfield's reactions to Dracula when they first meet. Renfield is "apprehensive," "uncomfortable" and

Edward Van Sloan and David Manners discover the coffin of Count Dracula (Bela Lugosi) in *Dracula*.

food to him, like the flower girl that he accosts on the foggy streets of London. He has no interest in such women. He approaches them, exerts his hypnotic control over them, sucks their blood and leaves them for dead. Dracula doesn't waste time trying to woo or seduce someone like that flower girl.

Then there are the women that he seeks for his brides. Women like Lucy and Mina. Dracula's approach toward these women is entirely different. He plays a game with them. He approaches them as if he were a human, gradually drawing them into his world. He seduces them first by force of his personality. Only after they've become intrigued with him, when they're already a bit hooked, does he approach them as a vampire. The process of vampirizing his victims is a gradual one. It climaxes in the mixing of Dracula's blood with his victim's. For those victims he wants to bring back as vampires, he opens up a vein, and has them drink his blood. Most of Dracula's victims don't come back as vampires (the flower girl; the crew of the *Vespa*). When they die they stay dead. Dracula's vampire brides must want to join him, if only ever so slightly, in the world of the undead.

Lucy, who is not put off by Dracula's odd manner, has a taste for the morbid. She's the one who recites the toast "Lofty timbres; the walls around are bare; echoing to our laughter as though the dead were there; Quaff a cup to the

"nervous." He makes efforts to conceal his "confusion" and "uneasiness." He wonders about his "weird host." True, Dracula is making little effort to conceal his true nature from Renfield. But even when Dracula is making an effort to pass as human, he doesn't or can't conceal his unusual qualities. His first meeting with Dr. Seward, his daughter Mina, Lucy Weston (Frances Dade) and Jonathan Harker (David Manners) in the opera house in London shows this. As their conversation progresses, becoming more and more morbid, everyone in that opera box (except for Lucy, who is fascinated by the Count) is made uncomfortable by Dracula. When he starts saying things like "To die, to be really dead, that must be glorious" and "There are far worse things awaiting man than death," it's as if he's just flung a dead armadillo into the opera box. As described in the shooting script, "Everybody looks at everybody else—a sudden feeling of constraint falls over them—no one speaks for a moment..." Everyone is relieved when the lights go down and they can turn their attention away from Dracula and back toward the stage.

In London we see how Dracula *courts* his women. Dracula approaches women in two very different ways. Some women are just

**The three brides of Dracula wander in Carfax Abbey in *Dracula*.**

dead already! Hurrah for the next who dies!" This prompts Dracula's odd observations on the nature of death.

Before going to bed that night, Mina teases Lucy about her infatuation with Count Dracula, even addressing her as "countess." Lucy has fallen hard for Count Dracula. Dracula's seduction of Lucy is effortless, so he wastes little time in coming on to her as a vampire.

While Lucy is an easy conquest for Dracula, Mina is another matter. Mina appears to have no dark side. She chides Lucy for bringing up that morbid toast. Later that night, Mina mocks Count Dracula (doing a passable imitation of the Count). As far as Mina is concerned, Lucy can have Count Dracula: "Give me someone a little more normal," she says.

For Dracula, Mina is a challenge. He wants to entice this bright, cheery girl into his world of

**Gloria Holden burns the body of Count Dracula (a dummy, not Bela Lugosi) in *Dracula's Daughter*.**

the undead. Mina is the equivalent of the virtuous woman that the roué seeks to deflower. She represents a challenge, a potential conquest and, ultimately, a testament to the seducer's power over women.

At the same time that Dracula has been vampirizing Lucy, he's been paying social calls on the Sewards. He's been telling Mina "some rather grim tales" of Transylvania (Vlad the Impaler stories, perhaps?). Mina may not like these types of stories, but she hasn't been rebuffing Count Dracula either. Perhaps she is just being polite to her new neighbor. Or, perhaps Mina has a hidden dark side, a side that Dracula brings out. Dracula has been gradually preparing Mina for the night he will come to her and complete his act of seduction.

Dracula plays these games with his victims because he is supremely confident that he will prevail. He can afford these little diversions because he is almost always in command of the situation. The one scene in *Dracula* when the Count loses control occurs when Van Helsing (Edward Van Sloan) confronts him with the mirror in the cigarette box. Dracula slams the box to the floor. Even in this scene, Dracula recovers his composure fairly rapidly.

Later, Dracula again confronts Van Helsing. It is clear that Dracula has rarely encountered such a formidable opponent. Few men in the world are any sort of match for Dracula. When Dracula attempts to put Van Helsing under his hypnotic power, Van Helsing, in a fierce struggle of wills, manages to resist. Dracula is impressed, telling Van Helsing, "Your will is strong."

Van Helsing is one human that Dracula can't play for a fool—something that Dracula enjoys doing. He likes playing cat and mouse games, or as he might term it, spider and fly games. He enjoys making private little jokes at the expense of the humans around him ("I never drink... wine.").

Dracula is a commanding, dominating personality. He makes little or no effort to blend in with his environment. Dracula is a seducer, bringing his prospective brides over to his world of the undead before he actually turns them into vampires. Dracula is almost always in a dominant position over his human adversaries. He rarely encounters a human being such as Van Helsing who is a match for him. But even Van Helsing couldn't dream of dominating Dracula, only of managing to defeat him. All of this allows Dracula to approach his vampiric work with a sense of fun.

These are the character traits of the true Dracula. And these vry specific traits are almost wholly absent from those two would-be Draculas, Count Alucard and Baron Latos.

### COUNT ALUCARD
*Son of Dracula* (1943)

Count Alucard is so unlike Count Dracula that it's hard to know where to begin. Perhaps the best place to start is with the title of the movie, *Son of Dracula*. It could have been called *The Return of Dracula*, or, even more appropriately, *Kay Caldwell, Vampire*. But it isn't. It's called *Son of Dracula*. Maybe he's the biological son of the human Dracula who, like his father, became a vampire. Maybe he's a human vampirized by Dracula, thus becoming his "son." Either way, the title of the movie is inescapable. Whoever Count Alucard is, he's certainly not Count Dracula.

**Lon Chaney, Jr. as Count Alucard from *Son of Dracula***

Count Alucard has none of the manners of a well-bred gentleman. He's rude, peremptory and openly contemptuous of the humans he meets. Alucard is not the least bit charming, not even when he's trying to be. When he puts his charm on Kay (Louise Albritton), such sizzle is obviously having little effect. She's off in another world, barely noticing him. Women are not attracted to Count Alucard. Kay's sister Clair (Evelyn Ankers) is probably speaking for most women when she says, "There's something rather repulsive about him."

Count Alucard's repellant qualities, including his distinct lack of sex appeal, explain why he is so easily manipulated by Kay. As far as Alucard is concerned, Kay is the best thing that's ever happened to him. She's a beautiful woman who loves him and longs to be a vampire. Alucard will do anything for Kay. He even, in a comically un-Dracula-like scene, takes her to a justice of the peace so they can be legally married.

The true Dracula would never marry one of his brides. In *Dracula*, the Count maintains a little harem... he keeps three brides in Castle Dracula. He's working on two others in Carfax Abbey. Monogamy is simply not a trait associated with Count Dracula; Dracula is the ultimate seducer. In *Son of Dracula*, Kay has seduced Alucard. Not only has she seduced him, she plays him for a sap! Kay is just using Alucard in a scheme to allow Kay and Frank (Robert Paige) to be vampire lovers forever. It is inconceivable that the real Count Dracula would allow himself to be used by a human in this way.

Count Alucard is a weak vampire, easily manipulated by the human Kay. But he's a weak vampire in other ways as well. Alucard has no mind control powers, or at least he doesn't use any in the course of the movie. And in one key moment he could have employed them. At one point Frank threatens Alucard with a gun. Although the gun can't harm Alucard, it could harm Kay. The true Dracula, in this scene, would have brought weak-willed Frank under his hypnotic control. Instead, Alucard does nothing. He just stands there and lets Frank fire away, killing Kay in the process. Maybe he should have borrowed his sister's Dracula ring. That seems to be useful for hypnotizing people.

In addition to being a weak vampire, Count Alucard is somewhat dimwitted. He's blissfully oblivious to Kay's schemes against him. And Alucard does stupid things. For example, the alias he picks for himself... is he trying to hide his supposed identity from people or advertise it? Count Alucard? It takes Dr. Brewster (Frank Craven), who has no particular interest in vampires, about 10 seconds to figure out that Alucard is Dracula spelled backwards. Alucard might as well call himself Dr. Acula.

**The weak dimwitted vampire from *Son of Dracula***

Alucard does even worse when he's forced to think on his feet. The aforementioned scene when he just stands still and lets Frank shoot up the place. And then there's the climax of the movie when he discovers his coffin in flames. He tries to put out the fire by hitting the coffin with a board. That will only fan the flames and make the fire that much more intense. His next tactic is to threaten the guy who lit the fire, an equally futile effort. Alucard is too panicky at this point to think straight. If he'd kept his wits about him, it might have occurred to him to whip off his cape and use it to smother the flames. Dracula should never be so panicky and desperate, no matter what the situation. Dracula didn't become King of the Vampires by having a propensity to lose his head in difficult circumstances.

Lon Chaney, Jr. and Robert Paige (Frank) from *Son of Dracula*

On the other side of the equation, Count Alucard does have one trait similar to the original Count Dracula. People do find him to be unsettling. The servant who answers the door when Alucard arrives at the plantation and the justice of the peace when he and Kay arrive both give a little start when they first see the Count. And Lon Chaney, Jr. is listed as "Count Dracula" in the film's credits. Given the evidence of the film itself, not to mention its title, these are slender reeds on which to pin Dracula-hood on Count Alucard.

## BARON LATOS
*House of Frankenstein* (1944)
*House of Dracula* (1945)

*House of Frankenstein* does not pick up the Dracula story where either *Dracula's Daughter* or *Son of Dracula* left off. Professor Lampini is displaying the "Actual Skeleton of Count Dracula" in his traveling Chamber of Horrors. According to Lampini, he recovered the skeleton "from the cellar of Dracula's castle in the Carpathian Mountains."

A good story, except that the original Count Dracula was in London when he was staked. Furthermore, Countess Zaleska cremated his body in *Dracula's Daughter*. A stake was not driven through Count Alucard's heart, instead he was destroyed by exposure to sunlight and was nowhere near the Carpathians at the time.

Whatever Lampini found in Castle Dracula, it wasn't the remains of either Count Dracula or his son. The only vampiric remains that we know of in Castle Dracula are those of Countess Zaleska, who was killed by an arrow on the family estate.

Lampini's vampire in the coffin with the Dracula crest is a Dracula wannabe. Baron Latos, the name he goes under, is closer to the original Count Dracula than the hapless Count Alucard. He has the bearing of a true aristocrat, and he's a more powerful vampire than Alucard. But, even so, he's a weak imitation of the original.

When we first see Latos, Dr. Niemann (Boris Karloff) has removed the stake from the skeleton and Latos has rematerialized. As Niemann holds the stake over Baron Latos' heart, Latos attempts to exert hypnotic control over Niemann. He commands Niemann to "Drop the stake from your hand... Drop it." Niemann at first wavers, but he resists Latos' will. Niemann is certainly a strong-willed character; he may be the equal to Van Helsing in that regard. But for Van Helsing, resisting Dracula's will was a huge effort, leaving him exhausted afterwards. For Niemann, it's almost effortless.

Niemann then makes a deal with Latos. If Latos will help him, Niemann will protect Latos during the daylight hours. Latos says, "For that, I will do whatever you wish." Count Dracula would never allow himself to be in a subservient position to a human being. Nor would he entrust the protection of his coffin by day to a strong-willed person with a personal agenda. The humans who serve Count Dracula are his slaves. In *House of Frankenstein* that relationship is reversed. Latos is Niemann's slave.

Later that night, Latos carries out his part of Niemann's bargain. He makes the acquaintance of Herr Hussman (Sig Ruman), delivering Niemann's revenge by killing him. Latos spends virtually the entire night with Herr Hussman, his son Carl (Peter Coe) and his daughter-in-law Rita (Anne Gwynne). They chat and drink wine until almost dawn (Baron Latos does drink... wine.). During this long evening, no one in the Hussman party

Dr. Edelmann (Onslow Stevens) and Baron Latos (John Carradine) from *House of Dracula*

toward his coffin but is destroyed by sunlight within hours of his being revived from his undead limbo.

One cannot imagine the real Count Dracula being so sloppy, so careless, so easily dispatched.

Baron Latos has been in undead limbo for many years. He hasn't feasted in quite a long time. Perhaps Baron Latos' distinct lack of formidability in *House of Frankenstein* is due to his weakened state. Baron Latos has no such excuse in *House of Dracula*. In this film, Latos is at the height of his powers. Yet, even here, he makes misjudgments that the true Count Dracula would never make. Most inexcusably, Baron Latos once again entrusts his daycare to a man that he cannot trust. Dr. Edelmann (Onslow Stevens) is a deeply religious man, strong-willed, who would never willingly serve Dracula. Why Baron Latos chooses to place his coffin in the cellar of Edelmann's castle and show Edelmann where it is (explaining to Edelmann just what he would have to do to destroy Baron Latos) is anyone's guess.

It's difficult to understand Baron Latos' motives in *House of Dracula*. Is Latos sincere when he comes to Dr. Edelmann seeking a cure, or is this just a ruse to gain has any sense of uneasiness or nervousness around Baron Latos. He seems to them exactly what he appears to be, a sophisticated, charming, Old-World aristocrat. He arouses no apprehensions. Nothing unusual stands out about this man. Only after the rest of the party retires, and Latos is alone with Rita, does Latos' other side come out.

Latos is unable, through force of his will alone, to hypnotize Rita. He relies on the Dracula ring to do it. He's also far too hasty in putting Rita under his hypnotic control and trying to abduct her. Possibly, Baron Latos is rushing things because he has little time. As the featured attraction in a traveling show, he can't bother with the niceties of seduction. Even so, he goes about it in a remarkably clumsy manner. After wasting most of the night socializing with his victims, he kills Hussman and abducts the girl just before dawn.

Carl discovers Hussman's body, sees that Rita is missing and immediately summons the police. Inspector Arnz (Lionel Atwill) and his men pursue Latos. With the gendarmes behind him and Niemann in front of him, Latos is trapped. At the first sign of trouble, Niemann breaks his side of the bargain with Latos and casts his coffin out of the caravan. Latos crawls desperately

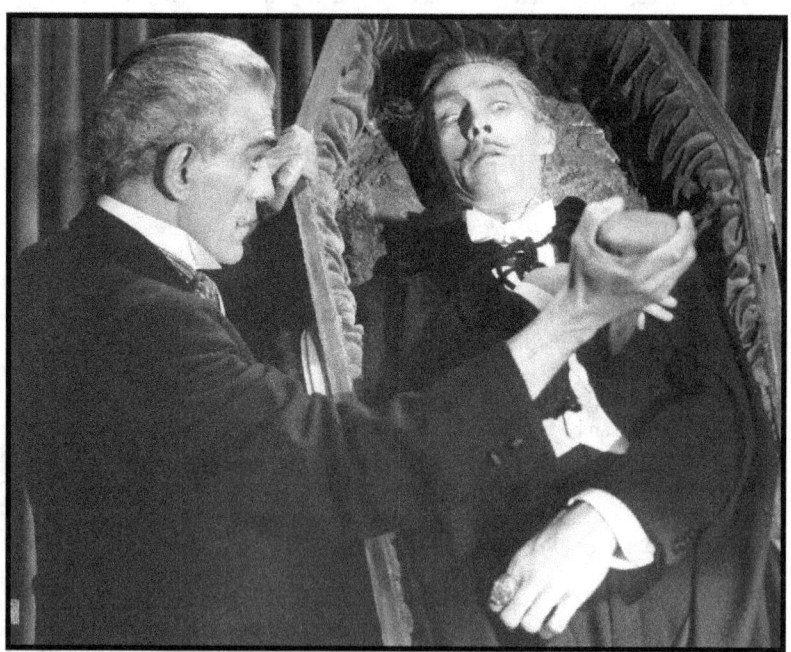

**Niemann (Boris Karloff) confronts Latos with a wooden stake.**

access to Edelmann's household? Latos formerly met Edelmann's nurse, Miliza (Martha O'Driscoll), in Bistritz. It's apparent that his primary motivation in coming to Visaria is to win Miliza. But does he plan to bring her into *his* world of the undead, or does he seek to join Miliza in *her* world of the living?

I believe that Latos is sincerely seeking a cure for his vampirism. If his seeking a cure is a ruse, it's an awfully elaborate and unnecessary one. Latos, as we've seen in *House of Frankenstein*, has no difficulty insinuating himself into the households of his human victims. The Hussmans gladly welcomed him into their house as a guest. Baron Latos is similarly unremarkable to the people he meets in *House of Dracula*. Miliza and Nina (Jane Adams) see nothing peculiar about him. Latos' nighttime appointments or singular blood condition do not seem to tip Nina off, and she knows a thing or two about vampires. He's already met Miliza socially. It would be an easy matter for the Baron to temporarily relocate to Visaria, pay social calls on Miliza and vampirize her when the time is ripe.

The suave and sophisticated Baron Latos from *House of Dracula*

As the treatment is nearing its end, at the point in the film when it is clear that Latos has decided not to go through with the cure, Dr. Edelmann comments on an anomaly he's discovered in Latos' blood samples. Latos responds, "Why worry so long as the treatments are proving successful." In the shooting script for *House of Dracula*, this line of dialogue is accompanied with the direction "dissembling." His dialogue in these later scenes is not supposed to be sincere. In his earlier scenes with Edelmann, no such direction accompanies his dialogue.

Why, with Edelmann on the verge of a cure, does Latos turn on his benefactor? I would postulate the answer in two words: Larry Talbot (Lon Chaney).

When Larry Talbot arrives at Edelmann's castle, it is clear that Miliza is taken with him. Should Edelmann succeed in finding a cure for Talbot, nothing would prevent Larry and Miliza from walking off together, hand in hand (as they ultimately do). The scene when Latos comes to Miliza, hypnotizes her and attempts to vampirize her, occurs after Talbot has attempted to kill himself. This suicide attempt ironically helps Edelmann to discover more of the spores necessary to operate on Talbot. All of this happens at night, when Latos would have been up and about. He must know what was going on with Talbot, Meliza and the spores. Miliza's concern for Talbot, and the prospect of a cure for him, would make it clear to Latos that Miliza would reject him in favor of Talbot. Once he realizes this, Latos gives up on his cure and reverts to type. This explains why Latos changes his mind. It also explains why Latos mixes his blood with Edelmann's; it's Latos' little revenge on Talbot.

This interpretation of *House of Dracula* is hardly conclusive. As Dr. Edelmann would say, "The whole thing is of a highly speculative nature." But it does account for Latos' behavior in the film. Either way, ruse or sincere, the Baron is no competition for Larry Talbot in *House of Dracula*. Baron Latos is not repellent to women, as Count Alucard is, but he just doesn't have the way with women that Count Dracula does.

Latos engages in some very un-Dracula-like behavior in *House of Dracula*. He willingly puts himself at the mercy of a human being. He does this for the sake of a woman who has little interest in him. Miliza prefers werewolves to vampires, thank you very much. Baron Latos is suave, debonair and sophisticated. But, in both *House of Frankenstein* and *House of Dracula,* he has a too trusting nature and puts himself at risk for a woman. In the end, in spite of his sophistication and suavity, Baron Latos is as hapless a vampire as Count Alucard.

### DR. LEJOS
*Abbott and Costello Meet Frankenstein* (1948)

Some questions linger as to whether *Abbott and Costello Meet Frankenstein* should be considered part of the official Universal Dracula/Frankenstein/Wolf Man series. It's a comedy and it doesn't pick up on any storylines left over from the earlier films. Despite this, I believe that *Abbott and Costello Meet Frankenstein* should be considered the final entry in the series. It wouldn't be the first Universal sequel that doesn't pick up from the previous

**The aging Bela Lugosi can still play romantic as Dr. Lejos in *Abbott and Costello Meet Frankenstein*.**

film. *Son of Dracula* has no connection to the first two Dracula movies. It's never explained why Larry Talbot, shot by a silver bullet at the end of *House of Frankenstein*, is alive and well at the beginning of *House of Dracula*.

As for its being a comedy, Universal horror films have had comic elements from the very beginning. Sometimes they are provided by laborers on the periphery of the film, such as Martin, the orderly in *Dracula*, or Minnie the maid in *Bride of Frankenstein*. Shipping clerks Chick Young (Bud Abbott) and Wilbur Grey (Lou Costello) are comic relief laborers in the tradition of Martin and Minnie. The only difference is that *Abbott and Costello Meet Frankenstein* puts the comedic characters at center stage, while relegating the romantic leads to the sidelines.

In *Abbott and Costello Meet Frankenstein*, the Dracula character goes by the alias of Dr. Lejos (Bela Lugosi). Interestingly, when Mr. McDougall (Frank Ferguson) arrives at the shipping office to pick up his exhibits, he describes one of the exhibits as "the remains of the original Count Dracula." This may be a subtle hint that the other Count Draculas that we've encountered in recent Universal films are *not* the original Count Dracula. Or it may be a sly reference to the return of Bela Lugosi to the role, after a 17-year absence.

It's tempting to say that, by virtue of the return of Lugosi to the role, Dr. Lejos must be the original Count Dracula. But there is other evidence in the film besides the casting of Lugosi that suggests that Dr. Lejos is the true Count Dracula.

This is the first movie since *Dracula* in which Dracula is in a commanding, dominating position. He's not under the thumb of a femme fatale or a mad scientist. Dr. Mornay (Lenore Aubert) is both a femme fatale *and* a mad scientist, but she's no match for Dr. Lejos. She balks at performing the brain operation on the Monster (Glenn Strange), foolishly thinking that she has the upper hand over Dr. Lejos. Lejos commands her to look into his eyes. She attempts to resist, but cannot. Dr. Mornay is utterly helpless before Dr. Lejos. After he vampirizes her, Dr. Mornay is suitably subservient to her master.

**Dr. Lejos in total command**

Not since Renfield, back in 1931, had a character addressed Dracula as "Master." In *Abbott and Costello Meet Frankenstein* two characters address him this way: Dr. Mornay and The Frankenstein Monster. This hardly seems coincidental. Dr. Lejos is the first Dracula since the original Count who actually acts as if he is someone's master. Dr. Lejos is a powerful vampire who commands, and receives, unquestioning obedience from those who serve him. More often than not, those other so-called Draculas are pawns, carrying out the schemes of others. Dr. Lejos is no one's pawn.

Dr. Lejos knows exactly what he wants and is methodical in carrying out his plans. He makes very few mistakes. He's undone not by his own weakness or incompetence, but by the unexpected intervention of a worthy adversary. Count Dracula could not have anticipated that the Sewards would obtain the help of

**Dr. Lejos poses in dramatic stance with Lou Costello from *Abbott and Costello Meet Frankenstein.***

Dr. Van Helsing. Dr. Lejos could not have anticipated that his plans would be thwarted by another creature of the night, Larry Talbot, the Wolf Man. In the climactic battle in the lab, the shooting script says, "Dracula turns, sees the Wolf Man bearing down on him. For the first time he reacts with fear." The humans in the film are no match for Dracula. But another supernatural creature can upset his plans.

Just like the true Dracula, Lejos is all smiles during social occasions. Count Alucard and Baron Latos, with

three films between them, virtually never smile. Dr. Lejos smiles constantly. Dr. Lejos enjoys his own private little jokes. He shows up at the masquerade party dressed as Dracula. He says of Wilbur, "What we need today is young blood… and brains" (Wilbur's brain, of course, is slated to be relocated into the body of the Monster). Dr. Lejos is enjoying himself immensely—as Count Dracula enjoys himself in *Dracula*. The same cannot be said of Count Alucard or Baron Latos in their respective films.

We don't see Dracula courting women in this movie. He's only just arrived in the United States, and he has bigger plans in mind at first. But, we do see him completely dominating his human adversaries, having fun with his little in-jokes, and playing the role of a charming, if somewhat odd, host.

Does all of this mean that Dr. Lejos is the original, true, one and only, Count Dracula?

Hell yes, it does!

Sources:

*MagicImage Filmbooks Presents: Abbott and Costello Meet Frankenstein,* Philip Riley, editor (Absecon, NJ: MagicImage Filmbooks, 1990).

*MagicImage Filmbooks Presents: Dracula: The Original 1931 Shooting Script,* Philip Riley, editor (Absecon, NJ: MagImage Filmbooks, 1990).

*MagicImage Filmbooks Presents: House of Dracula: The Original 1945 Shooting Script,* Philip Riley, editor (Absecon, NJ: MagicImage Filmbooks, 1993).

*MagicImage Filmbooks Presents: House of Frankenstein: The Original 1944 Shooting Script,* Philip Riley, editor (Absecon, NJ: MagicImage Filmbooks, 1990).

# NEW FROM MIDNIGHT MARQUEE PRESS, INC.

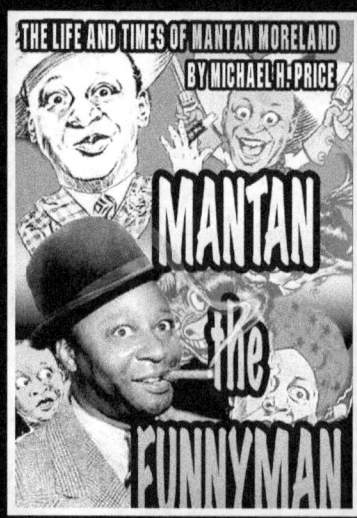

## 5 for $100

**5 for $100 or individually:**
**Forgotten Horrors 4**
by Michael H. Price
and John Wooley $25
**Mantan the Funnyman (w/CD)**
by Michael H. Price $35
**Alfred Hitchcock's London**
by Gary Giblin $25
**Good Movies: Bad Timing**
by Nicholas Anez $25
**You're Not Old Enough Son**
by Barry Atkinson $25

To order send a check or money order to:
Midnight Marquee Press, Inc.
9721 Britinay Lane
Baltimore, MD 21234
for credit card orders
call 410-665-1198
(9 a.m. - 6 p.m. EST)
or visit our website
www.midmar.com
for easy ordering

Shipping: $5 for first book  $1.00 for each additional

# DVD REVIEWS

*by Gary J. Svchla*

**Ratings: Excellent 4; Good 3; Fair 2; Poor 1**

**Voodoo Island
The Four Skulls of
Jonathan Drake**
Movie: *Voodoo*: 2.0; *Skulls*: 2.5;
Disc: 3.5
[MGM]

For a minimal cost of $15, MGM presents two B programmers remastered in pristine detail and the sparkling black and white reproduction rivals Criterion mastering. Extras include a trailer or two. Keeping the cost low and the restoration quality high is all I will ever ask.

*Voodoo Island* is a juvenile horror romp produced by Bel-Air Productions in 1957 (the same production team who made *The Black Sleep* and *The Pharaoh's Curse*), and even with icon horror king Boris Karloff, *Voodoo Island* is pretty mediocre. Most voodoo features are deadly dull, with a few exceptions, but this movie features Karloff as a debunker of the supernatural who disproves paranormal experiences with scientific explanations. In this case a huge hotel chain wants to expand on a supposedly haunted island when one man returns zombified, the rest of his party dead. Karloff takes a crew and the zombified human back to the island to discover the truth. One crewmember is Elisha Cook, Jr. who would sell his own mother for a buck. Karloff looks to the trip as somewhat of a vacation.

A few genuine eerie sequences appear. As the Karloff party is about to board its private plane, the mindless man stumbles past a little girl sitting quietly and sewing a face on her rag doll. The zombie twitches and half closes its eyes as the child thrusts her needle into the doll's head. Later, while on the island where natives lurk in the brush only a few feet from the unsuspecting visitors, carnivorous plants (well executed inflatable rubber plants) attack unsuspecting victims by slamming down upon them. A few of these sequences are quite spooky and cause some sudden jumps. In related sequences one dumb blonde strips and jumps into

the nearby river, unaware that these phallic predator plants are waiting nearby to shield the unmentionable areas of her nude form from audience gawking, as well as sucking out her life's energy. In another chilling sequence a member of the Karloff party watches as two tribal children play in the jungle (the first sign of life) when one child is totally absorbed by a giant Venus Fly Trap-derived plant. The man watches in horror, the shock quickly reducing him to a zombie state.

But too much of *Voodoo Island* is lethargic and slow-moving. The characters are well drawn and are interesting; most characters have tainted pasts and so much to forget! Stereotypes perhaps, but highly interesting ones. And Boris Karloff, not recreating a demented Dr. Frankenstein, plays a cantankerous human being for a change. Not a particularly well-defined role, but still a regular old-timer with gusto and energy. *Voodoo Island* is never better than mediocre, but as reproduced here in such a pristine presentation, it is well worth checking out again.

The second feature, *The Four Skulls of Jonathan Drake*, was a perennial favorite of mine back in the early 1960s when local neighborhood theaters were still running this film theatrically. I loved it to death and remember it fondly. I remember when vacationing in Wildwood, New Jersey (an ocean beach resort), I walked the boardwalk to travel to a novelty shop that sold rubber shrunken heads, something I had to have after devouring this movie. Alas, the film does not hold up very well and what mesmerized and spooked a 12-year-old boy has lost that old black magic when viewed today.

However, Henry Daniell, in one of his final roles, is spectacular as the evil doctor/voodoo high priest who is seeking revenge on generations of the Drake family. The Drake men all seem to die from heart attacks exactly at age 60. Eduard Franz portrays latest victim-to-be Jonathan and his repartee with Daniell is classic. During the film's climax, it is revealed that Daniell's character has a black body

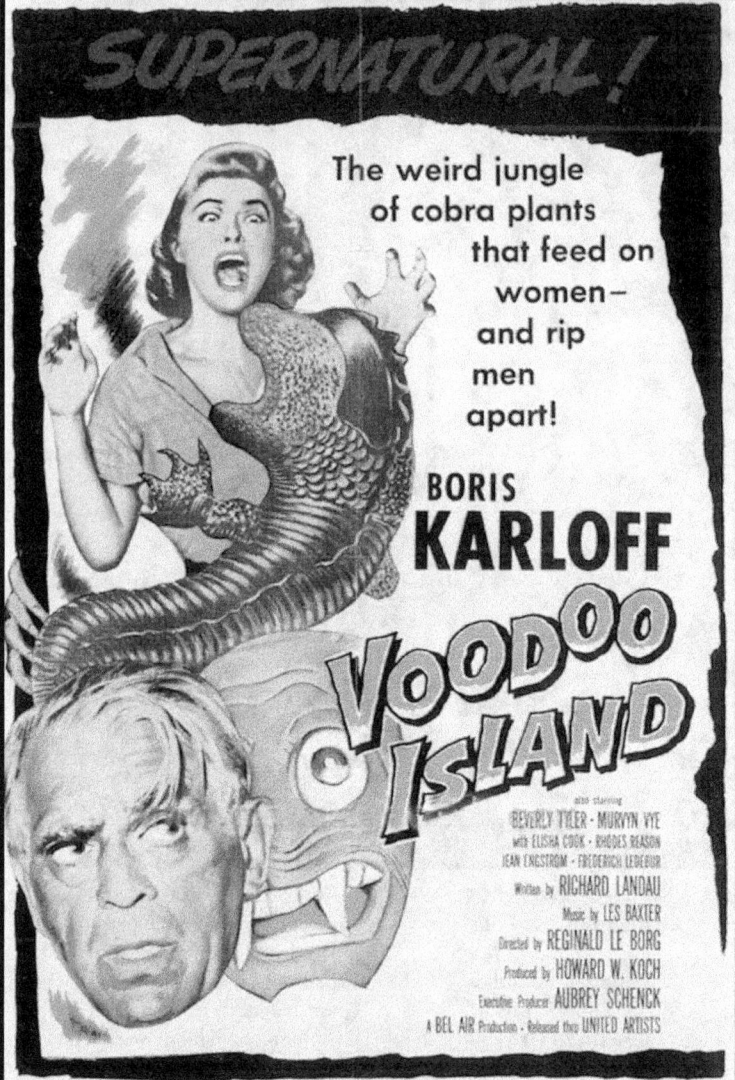

with a sewn-on Caucasian head. And his henchman, decked out in jungle uniform and Prince Valiant hairstyle, appears to be a gigantic version of a classic shrunken head. However, the face of actor Paul Wexler makes him appear to be a voodoo native straight out of New Jersey (Wexler did portray Grissom the butler in *The Bowery Boys Meet the Monsters*). But Wexler's character is eerie and chilling, except in his final climactic knife battle when his long blade wiggles and looks just like the rubber fake it is.

Under Edward Cahn's effective direction, several sequences linger in the viewer's mind. The Paul Wexler character hiding in the shadows, who then approaches the brother of Jonathan Drake and so skillfully dabs his poison-tipped blade into the soft tissue of the victim's neck, drawing only a speck of blood. Within seconds Drake collapses and is dead, as the voodoo native quickly cuts off his head and escapes into the estate yard. The sequence where Henry Daniell takes the dead man's head and reduces it to the iconic shrunken head is masterfully photographed, with the boiling flesh and sewing of orifices shut quite shocking for 1959 B productions. And that sequence lingered in my imagination and dreams for several years.

While *The Four Skulls of Jonathan Drake* and *Voodoo Island* are

perhaps the nadir of the zombie/voodoo genre, each film has something to recommend it. Presented as double features at a discount price with fabulous original source material, both films warrant a chuckle, a chill and a warm smile reliving the cinematic past of our youth.

### Boogeyman
Movie: 2.0; Disc: 3.5
[Sony]

Sam Raimi's Ghost House Pictures, his low-budget horror film production company, is a clever way of keeping his finger on the pulse of his past, staying attached to the low-budget horror film roots where he got his start. Director Stephen Kay's *Boogeyman* is an exercise in creating nail-biting horror, but it ultimately comes off more as exercise than as a total movie. This would have made a fantastic half-hour audition DVD, but for 89 minutes it seems almost too long for what little story and character development it offers. The movie is concocted as almost a one-character show, but star Barry Watson does not quite convey all the internal turmoil he has to endure. As a child he has visions of the Boogeyman occupying his bedroom closet or causing evil manifestations using innocent objects from his room (clothes piled on a chair, a flying model bird overhead, an action figure on his shelf, etc.). However, when his father appears to assure his son that an over-active imagination is the cause of his visions and restlessness, the father is violently taken and banged against the bedroom walls and pulled into the closet, never to be seen again. The movie picks up 15 years later with the funeral of Jim's (Barry Watson) whacked-out mother and his return to his former family home, where the nightmares (which still haunt) continue. Along for the ride are the uncle who raised him and two women in his life, the sultry rich bitch blonde who seems to use Tim as a means to affront her family's sensibilities, and the down home girl from the old neighborhood who never married and still has the hots for Tim. The movie is little more than vignettes showcasing the evils of the house and Tim's slowly blooming courage facing his demons.

In perhaps one of the movie's finest sequences, his blonde girlfriend convinces Tim to "have some fun" sexually, as she prepares by taking a bath (not a shower) in preparation in their motel room. After Tim returns to find the tub empty with only a bloody handprint on the tub's rim, we soon find the tub filling rapidly with bloody water and the CGI-morphed naked blonde seems to be totally in the evil possession of the Boogeyman, whose human form morphs out of the bloody water yanking the blonde victim too and fro. In this pivotal sequence, the water demon cradles the naked woman in his arms (revisiting the typical monster/heroine stance in any classic horror movie poster) before melding back into tub water, the blonde now gone forever. In another similarly intriguing sequence, Tim goes alone into his old home's bedroom closet and gets jerked around like a rag doll without benefit of any visible demon, the entire scene created with Watson's horrific reactions, booming sound editing and quick-cut visual editing that creates 20 seconds of pure horror. The entire movie becomes little more than a showcase for such sequences, well executed and delivered, but without much in the way of plot or character interaction. If direction Stephen Kay uses this talent integrated with effective plotting (interestingly enough, three writers take credit for the minimal screenplay) and character development, he might some day make an interesting picture. But, as stated earlier, *Boogeyman* is little more than an exercise in horror that is dependent

mostly upon cinematic trickery and a booming soundtrack that makes the horror angle too gimmicky and too easily created.

For fans that enjoy alternative endings (the alternative ending is more satisfying than the one used; the theatrical ending has Tim mutter "it's over" and the end credits come up without having created the sense that the horror is indeed defeated), deleted sequences and plenty of making-of documentaries, *Boogeyman* more than fills the bill here. Too bad the movie did not offer more substance.

### Saw
Movie: 3.0; Disc: 3.5
[Lions Gate]

Co-screenwriters and director Leigh Whannell and James Wan, who also appear in supporting performances in the movie, represent the enthusiasm and intelligence of independent movie making. *Saw* is totally original, possibly ranking with David Fincher's *Seven*, a film with which *Saw* shares some similarity. Even though the film was sold on the strength of its gore and mayhem, *Saw* is relatively gore-free. Yes, we do have some bloodied corpses, but the film's major payoff, where dejected Cary Elwes uses a hacksaw to cut off his foot to escape from his shackles, is handled with screams and cut-away shots. Gorehounds will be disappointed.

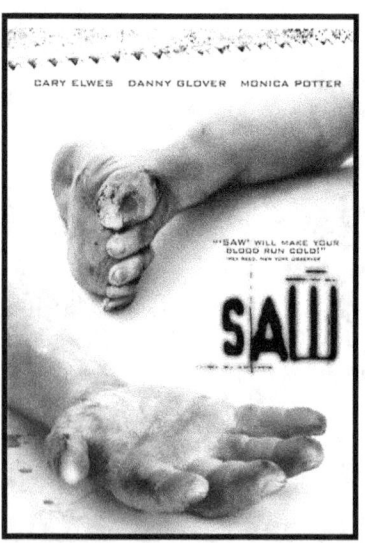

Fans of suspense cinema who love complicated and intelligent plots, something sadly missing from most of today's filmmaking, will perk up their eyes as this movie unfolds. Director James Wan demonstrates that brutal intensity can be delivered without showing the guts and grue. For instance, the Jigsaw killer has a young lady in a cellar, wearing a bear trap around her head and jaw. Once she moves away from the chair and the alarm is tripped, she has a short period of time to find the key to open the trap before it literally explodes, ripping the woman's jaw apart. The key, unfortunately, is buried deep within the stomach of a drugged-out male and a small knife lies near his unconscious body. She literally has to cut into stomach and intestines and use her hands to find the key to free herself. Yes, James Wan does show a few feet of intestines being fingered, but that's about the extent of the festivities, except for a few pints of blood.

Thrown into the mix is a dedicated and obsessed cop, Danny Glover, whose partner was killed by the Jigsaw killer after both officers trapped the fiend in his lair. Glover gets his throat slashed (but he does survive), but his younger partner walks into the killer's trap, trips a wire, and dies in a fury of shotgun blasts. Glover will not rest until he personally kills the fiend.

Cut to our major cast of characters... a doctor (Elwes) cheating on his wife is photographed by a private investigator. By the movie's beginning both of these men are shackled in a large filthy industrial bathroom with a bloody corpse sprawled between them, the victim of a self-inflicted gunshot wound to the head. Via cell-phone, the Jigsaw killer orders the doctor to murder the photographer

by 6 p.m. or his wife and child will be slaughtered.

Back at home, an orderly from work, a colleague of the good doctor, becomes the boogeyman in the closet who terrifies and ties up both the wife and little girl, but is he the Jigsaw killer or is he also under the gun to kill someone in order to save his worthless life? And is the corpse in the men's bathroom actually dead?

While a few holes exist in the plot, and a few sequences exist that would be better trimmed down slightly, this debuting feature by the team of Whannell and Wan is extremely impressive and the duo shows great future promise. *Saw* features nail-biting horror suspense (similar to *Silence of the Lambs*) of the most gripping variety. What distinguishes this movie is the fact that it is basically a character study of two men confined to one dirty little room and how they reveal their past lives and the demons that tilted their morality off the edge. Neither man is evil, but both men are flawed, and the Jigsaw killer's motives, teaching flawed humans the value of their lives, could only be taught by a person who knew he was losing the battle for his own.

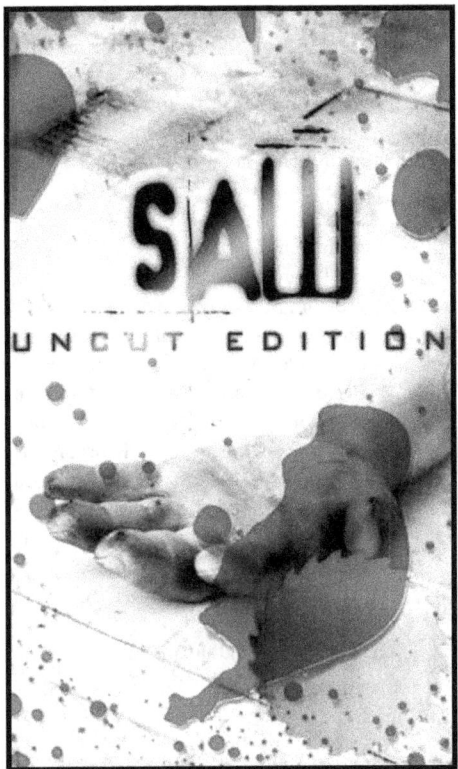

Not a film that audiences will watch time and time again, but *Saw* delivers the frightening goods packaged with wonderful performances and an intelligent script.

Extras include a DTS ES 6.1 and Dolby Digital 5.1 EX surround audio, documentaries, audio commentary, two music videos, trailers, still and poster gallery and a beautiful widescreen print.

**Panic in Year Zero**
**The Last Man on Earth**
Movie [*Panic*: 2.0; *Last Man* 2.0];
Disc: 3.5
[MGM]

This latest offering from MGM struck me as odd for a double-feature release. But the more I thought about both movies, the better sense the dual release made. First of all, both films were made in the early 1960s and released by American International. Both films deal thematically with the end of the world. Both films are filmed in widescreen black and white. So both *Panic in Year Zero* and *The Last Man on Earth* do complement one another.

To be honest, I never much enjoyed *Panic in Year Zero* when I saw it in 1962 upon its theatrical release. Where were the mutant monsters? Perhaps its apocalyptic message was simply a tad too sanitized yet potentially real, being released the same year as the Cuban Missile Crisis occurred. Now that we are 40 years removed from that too real threat of nuclear world destruction, audiences are better able to enjoy the film as the exploitation programmer it is. Ray Milland stars as the father who is taking his family on a vacation camping in the mountains. Along for the ride is wife Jean Hagen and children Frankie Avalon and Mary Mitchel. In the early morning hours, safely out of Los Angles, the family experiences what they believe are lightning strikes, which turn out to be a nuclear attack on the city, as a huge matte painting of a mushroom cloud hovers over the city. Year Zero, the end of one civilization and the beginning of a new one, with father Milland taking firm control, aided by dutiful son Frankie Avalon.

The communal panic is reflected by honking cars and trucks squeezing on down the highways in a crowded, herky-jerky fashion; however, the dim-witted Ray Milland family tries to swim upstream against exiting traffic to go back into Los Angeles, ultimately abandoning such a tame brain idea as they are continually forced off the road. We witness the family's frantic stops at roadside restaurants, the gauging of gas prices as service station owners dare to charge $9 per gallon instead of the regular 33 cents. We have Ray Milland and family wisely abandoning the main drags to hit a general store in a small rural town where they purchase hundreds of dollars of supplies, and then the owner calls up his friend who owns the hardware store and tells him to get over to the store fast, if he wants to make lots of money. However, the hardware store episode ends with Milland pointing the gun he is buying at the shop owner, who refuses to accept a personal check. This is not *On the Beach* but a quickly produced low-rent version of the end of the world.

The episodic film does feature a few dynamite sequences. The family has to cross a major congested road that is choked with traffic, and because of the panic, the constant flow of traffic will not lessen. At nightfall Milland uses a container of gasoline to create a firewall across the road, allowing his son and the family car to jump across while traffic is momentarily halted. In another sequence three teenage hoodlums force the Milland car off the road as the thugs threaten Milland and steal his wallet. Upon cue Milland shouts for his son to shoot one of the boys, but the shot goes slightly wide. Milland gets the drop on the teens and sends them on

their way. It turns out that mother Jean Hagen, upset at the prospect of her son killing another human being, shoved his arm at the instant he was firing his rifle, causing the crack shot to almost miss his target. However after the father gives his survival at any cost speech, even mother appears to fall into line. Later, while the family is camped in an isolated part of the woods, two of these same thugs corner and rape Milland's innocent teenage daughter in a harrowing scene for 1962. In the climax of the movie son Frankie Avalon is shot in the leg and loses plenty of blood, and while a community doctor can stop the bleeding and patch him up, the doctor states the son needs a transfusion within hours or he will die. So the race against time is on as father Milland looks for a larger town that will possess a blood supply.

Milland's direction is suspenseful and he keeps the tension building; however, with nary a script in sight, not even credible performances can carry all the dramatic weight. The photography is crisp and Les Baxter's blaring jazz score adds to the suspense. *Panic in Year Zero* is too realistic to appeal to sci-fi buffs, but it is too ridiculous to appeal to the general mainstream movie market. Bottom line, it is neither fish nor fowl and remains an A.I.P. anomaly.

Vincent Price was the superstar of American International horror when he went to Italy to film *The Last Man on Earth*, based upon Richard Matheson's classic horror novel *I Am Legend*. The movie is never better than fair, with an almost one-man performance that is simply not strong enough to carry the entire weight of the movie. The pedestrian direction by Ubaldo Ragona does not help. With a film noir narrative voice-over delivered by Price, the movie is sidelined by mediocre performances and bland cinematography. Just like *Panic in Year Zero*, the barren on-location streets become dull far too soon instead of evoking the mood of isolation. Many years after Hammer set the norm for bloody vampire stakings, the artistic decision for the camera to pull away as Morgan (Price) drives the stake home is disappointing to audiences who, in 1964, expected far more gore. The idea of a wind-borne worldwide plague is hammered home by strong autumn breezes and leaves carried across the backyard. Morgan's daughter, who sleeps under a net over her bed, gradually gets sick and goes blind and cries all through the night for her mommy, these being symptoms of the fatal plague. But when the wife also gets sick, as soon

as she goes blind she dies, while the daughter suffers in the blind state for several days. The willy-nilly Morgan pushes the vampire zombies around far too easily (thus making the vampires appear weak and less threatening) and Vincent Price seems positively uncomfortable doing the macho action hero routine.

When Morgan meets a surviving dog, his hopes rise and audiences expect real rapport to bloom between human and pet. However, the pet immediately runs away with Morgan in hot pursuit, and when the wounded dog returns to Morgan's home, the animal has been infected and must be destroyed. Thus this interesting plot thread is over as soon as it begins. And when Morgan eventually meets a human being who is still human, the woman's less-than-credible acting hinders the partnership that results. Surprisingly, it turns out the woman has been sent ahead to infiltrate Morgan's home, that she is an infected humans who takes a vaccine regularly to remain human. For some strange and unknown reason, such semi-humans, who can be cured by a transfusion of Morgan's blood, feel threatened by him and plan to kill him that night. Retreating to a church, in an over-dramatic visual metaphor, Price is shot and speared on the front altar screaming that he is the last man on Earth. And Morgan has been sacrificed so the new breed can live and start their new era as an ever-evolving race of former-humans.

In the too brief onscreen interview with author Richard Matheson that appears as a DVD extra, Matheson notes that no movie version ever got the novel right, and boy, was Matheson correct. *The Last Man on Earth* is indeed the best movie version of *I Am Legend*, but poor acting, bad dubbing, lethargic pacing and far too few memorable sequences compromise this bland production. Vincent Price does an admirable job as Morgan, but the flashback sequences of him at the lab at work and at home with his wife and daughter fail to capture the horror of a world-wide crisis with time running out. The vampire zombies are sometimes said to have been an inspiration for George Romero's zombies in 1968's *Night of the Living Dead*, and this may very well be true. However, Romero created more than just a look and a way of movement for his reanimated corpses, he created a sense of dread and intense horror. Just one scene showing Morgan push his way through the crowd of vampires and that illusion of horror dissipates immediately.

The widescreen 16:9 enhanced print is beautiful looking; however, a pristine print means little if the movie itself is totally mediocre. While it is wonderful to see such stunning transfers for both *Panic in Year Zero* and

*The Last Man on Earth*, it is just as sad to see that neither film transcends mediocre trappings.

**Jaws (30th Anniversary Edition)**
Movie: 3.5; Disc: 3.5
[Universal]

*Jaws* is a Steven Spielberg movie that I purposely avoided in the 30 years since its original release. After reviewing recent editions of *E.T. The Extra-Terrestrial* and *Close Encounters of the Third Kind*, I dreaded the thought that a marvelous movie that thrilled and chilled me back in 1975 would come off as disappointing today. In 1975 I loved *Jaws* and thought it was one of the scariest monster movies of the modern era.

Now the print has been restored with new 5.1 surround sound added (either Dolby or DTS), with a second disc of extras (including a two-hour documentary on the making of the film, production photos and posters, storyboards, etc.).

For once I can safely say that *Jaws* in 2006 is just as chilling and as much fun as it was back in 1975. Yes, the mechanical shark model, which was flawed and caused director Spielberg problems 30 years ago, looks perhaps even a little less realistic today. However, *Jaws* is not about the 25-foot mechanical model, and it never was. The movie shines best when cinematographer Bill Butler's camera becomes the subjective eyes of the beast and watches dangling legs and feet as humans might eye chicken wings. The film's opening sequence where cutie-pie Susan Blacklinie playfully strips and dives into the water, hoping to lure her boyfriend in to play, remains a classic. With her vulnerability encapsulated by her nudity, eyed from below, the shark approaches her vulnerable form, but she of course is unaware of any impending threat. Once the shark attacks (the viewer never sees the shark, we only see Blacklinie's reactions and hear her screams... all framed by John Williams' classic shark leifmotif), horror reigns as she gasps for breath, her eyes ablaze with fear and horror, as her body is jerked violently from side to side, then she is pulled silently underwater for the final time. This is the horror of *Jaws*! In another sequence scuba diver Richard Dreyfuss investigates a hole in a sunken boat in the dark, muddy waters. Suddenly the head of a corpse, its one eye missing, quietly floats into the scene illuminated by a flashlight, and the entire audience screams for its life. The most effective horror concocted by *Jaws* is the dread, the anticipation of horror that might be, as the silly humans ignore the warnings and only think about profits and losses and decide to keep the beaches open. That is, until that deadly fin appears in the children's safe-harbor pond and mayhem erupts.

And the film's absolute best sequence occurs on that small boat owned and manned by shark killer Quint (Robert Shaw), who is joined by scientist and shark expert Hooper (Dreyfuss) and Sheriff Brody (Roy Scheider), who admits to being afraid of boats and the water. In such a horrifying and claustrophobic setting, it is the character interaction that shines most brightly. The abrupt appearance of the shark as Brody throws chum into the sea sets the tone of horror. Quint, he with the unidentifiable accent and born a man of the sea, a lifelong sailor, contrasts nicely with the college-bred Hooper, also an expert on killer sharks, but a man who comes at his knowledge from an entirely different angle. Quint and Brody's pivotal bonding occurs as each man proudly rolls up a pant leg or shirt to reveal a scar worse than the one shown before. This masterful scene ends with both men, truly in fear for their lives, laughing hilariously, getting drunker each and every minute. The concerned Brody

constantly asks, "Ya think we need a bigger boat???!!!!" and remains terrified each waking moment. Brody becomes the Everyone of the movie, the character most of us are. Spielberg understands only too well that such harrowing scenes of horror only matter if the audience knows and cares about the characters being threatened. And on the climactic boat sequence, Spielberg's mastery as director, illustrated by the impending dread of when the shark will next appear, married to a complex character study, makes for classic moviemaking. The craven coward Brody becomes what appears to be the final survivor, as the boat is half sunk, but Brody cleverly feeds the shark an oxygen tank and then, at a safe distance, fires his rifle into the tank, exploding both it and the fiend. Quint, unfortunately, is dead, the victim of sliding down into the shark's jaws and being eaten alive, but Hooper survives his underwater scuba battle of cat and mouse and emerges safe and sound after the shark's destruction. Both courageous survivors carry on jovially as they paddle back to shore

Verna Fields' editing, Steven Spielberg's direction and the ensemble acting all combine to result in what has become a classic of horror, a wonderful monster movie to boot. Happily, *Jaws*, 30 years later, still remains one of Spielberg's best-realized films and is most definitely a modern movie classic.

**The Cat and the Canary**
Movie: 3.0; Disc: 3.5
[Image]

Magically, Image Entertainment discontinued its original issuing of this 1927 Universal old dark house murder mystery a few years ago anticipating this restored and remastered version. And the new release is, as expected, superior in every way.

Remember, German director Paul Leni both designed and directed the German Expressionistic classic *Waxworks* in 1924, and Universal's Carl Laemmle brought Leni to America to direct *The Cat and the Canary* in 1927, his first American film.

The print offered here is a dense 35mm print restored with tinted sequences intact. The audience is offered a choice of two musical scores, but Franklin Stover composed the excellent modern score.

*The Cat and the Canary* eludes style, even from the gloved hand that wipes the cobwebs from the wall revealing the title credits in a most haunting fashion. While Leni did not design the sets (Universal master Charles D. Hall did the honors here), his directorial style is always in evidence. In the film's opening montage crusty old Cyrus West—whose greedy relatives await his death and metaphorically become cats stalking a canary—is superimposed with giant milk bottles surrounding him and evil-eyed cats peering down upon him, as he tries to run from bottle to bottle, seeking refuge. Ultimately,

West slumps down into his chair and dies. West's final wish is that his will won't be read for 20 years, and when his only direct heir Annabelle West is named to inherit everything, the only stipulation is that if she is declared insane the estate will go to another named heir, whose name is sealed in a second envelope. During these opening sequences a furry cat-like hand holds the various envelopes. And the first moody sequences display a subjective walk down a long corridor, window curtains to the left blow in the wind, as a huge winding staircase lies at the end of the corridor. Just this establishing shot of West's now 20-year vacant house sets the tone for this old dark house mystery. On the night the will is to be read, we watch, via another subjective shot, as a twisting mysterious figure, using a flashlight (the scene is lit by the round circle of light cast by the flashlight), approaches a secret panel that hides a wall safe. His gloved hand opens the safe and re-deposits a sealed envelope, making it appear the safe was never opened. The lawyer reading the will arrives, an ominous figure in heavy cloak and hat, slightly bent over, banging heartily on the huge doorknocker, creating a sense of dread. When he soon opens the supposedly unopened safe, he catches a moth with his fingertips, becoming aware that someone already read the will recently. Even the creepy housekeeper, who lives alone, tells the lawyer she doesn't need the living ones, meaning human companionship is not necessary for her and she believes she lives with Cyrus' ghost.

The movie contains all the old chestnuts expected, but in 1927 the stage play and movie were relatively new. We have well-executed sequences showing the huge portrait of West hanging in the living room almost falling off the wall, startling the people assembled beneath it. In one subjective shot, from the point of view of the painting, the imposing figure of Cyrus West looks down upon all, who look up at him in terror. As the portrait finally falls and is retrieved by the gloomy housekeeper, she states something horrible will happen here tonight! And within minutes a husky guard enters the house and states he is on the lookout for an escaped lunatic (who thinks he's a cat and tears his victims apart) who was tracked to the mansion's gates. When the lawyer asks to see Annabelle alone, he offers to give her the envelope of the man who inherits everything if Annabelle is deemed insane. The lawyer tells her that the letter has been opened and that the person named within already knows he/she is second in line and could cause grave danger to Annabelle. As the lawyer speaks, in the background, the library shelf is slowly pushed forward, as a fiend emerges from the panel in back, his cat-clawed hand slowly reaching out for the lawyer's neck. "The name is..." the lawyer declares, as he is grabbed from behind and forced into the panel that suddenly closes.

When the Cat periodically appears, he is cloaked in a heavy coat and floppy hat, two huge fangs protruding upward from his bottom lip, a large plastic eye and rubber nose covering his own. It is a rather unique and minimal disguise that somehow works. At the film's climax, after attacking the hero in his underground lair and knocking him unconscious, the Cat sneaks back into the house proper and, creeping slowly up behind Annabelle, once again his cat-like hand lingers in the air above and behind her for an infinite period of time. He suddenly makes his presence known, as the recovering hero jumps into the fight to save the day. The Cat's disguise falls off during the melee and his identity is quickly revealed as the police arrive and give chase. The fiend's identity does not prove to be a surprise, but his performance, even once revealed, is unsettling and creepy.

Laura La Plante, as heiress Annabelle, is youthful yet surprisingly matronly and very proper. She does a fine job when required to be suspicious or terrified. Creighton Hale, as Paul, starts the movie as the comic coward, but by the middle of the film, after falling for Annabelle even before she becomes wealthy, he becomes her brave protector. The remainder of the cast are wonderful stereotypes and do a generally bang up job, even if Leni telegraphs a little too frequently the identity of the fiend. Produced only four years before *Dracula*, at Universal, *The Cat and the Canary* has a Germanic visual style with a ever-flowing camera that seems to imply, had Leni survived (he died in 1929 of blood poisoning), he might have been given the nod to direct *Dracula*, and oh, what a difference that might have made.

Besides the stunning restored print and musical scores, the DVD features a Harold Lloyd comic short, *Haunted Spooks*, whose haunted house theme nicely complements the main feature. And the title cards in *Haunted Spooks* are worth the price of admission. If Paul Leni had survived, his impact upon the world of Universal horror might have been profound, but his *Cat and the Canary* is a triumph of mood, photography and wonderful silent movie acting.

### The Village
Movie: 3.0; Disc: 3.5
[Buena Vista]

M. Night Shyamalan has directed himself into a box and apparently does not know how to escape. *The Sixth Sense* may very well be a modern horror film classic, and his immediate follow-up *Unbreakable*, while certainly not a classic, is still an excellent exercise in suspense and terror. But the patterns were already established by the production of these two films. Shyamalan created characters with deep psychological baggage that soon is revealed to be supernatural in nature, but such supernatural elements are disguised until the shocking payoff ending. And that's the Shyamalan gimmick—everything comes together during the final shock twist. Okay, for two films we can give the writer-director some creative slack. But then the disappointing *Signs* appeared, still filmed in Philadelphia but replacing Bruce Willis with Mel Gibson. *Signs* was quirky and unsettling, but it also meandered and suggested far more than the underwhelming payoff. The deeply troubled and psychologically driven Gibson character going up against the supernatural by way of an alien invasion was becoming far too familiar. Now, with *The Village* we once again visit the Philadelphia rural countryside, just like in *Signs*, with the same quasi-religious undertone, but this time delivered as a period piece occurring in 1897, introduced by the gravestone of a child's funeral at the film's beginning. Of course several deeply troubled individuals are saved by the show-stopping twist near the end.

Once again Shyamalan's one-trick pony has become blatant. Perhaps, as many suggest, the director needs to stop writing his own films and instead direct someone else's screenplay. But the bottom line remains that Shyamalan is a terrifically talented director with a keen visual eye whose movies are always character motivated, where human interaction matters more than visual effects and cheap shock. Perhaps Shyamalan has been bouncing off the walls of the box where he finds himself imprisoned, but once the crafty artist finds his new direction, I feel he will once again make movies as original and emotionally charged as *The Sixth Sense*.

To be fair, *The Village* is a better movie than *Signs* and is a step in the right direction. His cast, cushioned by talent such as John Hurt (in one of his finest performances of the last decade), Joaquin Phoenix, Adrian Brody and Sigourney Weaver, produces a terrific ensemble feel to the proceedings. However, the debuting performance by Bryce Dallas Howard (daughter of Ron Howard) is a star turn and a marvelous, deeply felt performance. Perhaps *The Village* may be forgotten in a decade, but Howard's performance, riveting and absolutely honest, will give the film the immortality for which it deserves to be remembered. Even though Shyamalan's screenplay is ultimately gimmicky and disappointing, when the film remains a period piece focused upon a relatively simple plot, the film is pure visual drama.

Isolated valley villagers are at truce with monsters that live beyond the woods, but in spite of the red-demon cloaked figures who mark the houses with blood and dead animals, blind Ivy (Howard) falls in love with reflective, withdrawn Lucious (Phoenix). However village idiot Noah (Brody), in blind rage and jealousy, stabs Lucious, leaving him for dead. Only by sending out the blind Ivy to go through the woods to the town that lies beyond can she fetch the medicine that may save Lucious' life. Ivy's ability to know her whereabouts immediately, her tender and transcendent face, with piercing eyes and her sense of being fearless, only show the extent of true love when she ventures alone on her journey, abandoned by two brave males who chicken out, ready to face the unknown, willing to face any demons (either internal or external) to save the life of her love. Howard's performance is Oscar worthy.

The sequence where the unwary Lucious is attacked by the mentally challenged Noah—who slides his long blade slowly into Lucious' gut with nary a reaction from the soon-to-collapse groom, accented only by the thud of the man's fall to the wooden floor—is an eerie sequence that chills the blood. Even more difficult to view is the follow-up scene where Noah bends down over the body and continues to stab the fallen innocent's torso, as the scene cuts away.

*The Village* contains marvelous extras including Bryce Howard's on location personal journal, deleted scenes, a documentary, another one of Shyamalan's home movies and a beautiful Dolby EX surround soundtrack. Most people will probably find the film's pacing slow and lethargic, but the character interaction kept me involved, that and all the wonderful performances, especially Bryce Dallas Howard's breakout one. Folks, this isn't *The Sixth Sense*, but *The Village* offers multiple payoffs for the patient viewer.

**The Alligator People**
Movie: 2.5; Disc: 3.5
[Fox]

Back in 1959, a B horror movie in black and white and CinemaScope was something rather special. Such a widescreen horror film with its denser, far-reaching tapestry of mood,

monsters and fright upped the ante of the production.

Roy Del Ruth, one of the oldest directors working in Hollywood at the time, created an old-style horror romp (even using Karl Struss as cinematographer) for the new pop art generation... men turned into alligators through the use of an alligator serum and a radiation machine created in an atomic laboratory. Old schoolers Frieda Inescort, Lon Chaney, Jr., George Macready and Bruce Bennett joined new upstarts Richard Crane (fresh from the *Rocky Jones* TV series) and Beverly Garland (most recently an American International heroine working for Roger Corman).

This programmer deals with dual losses of identity. First in the framing story, young and lovely Beverly Garland has repressed her former life of horror, and only through hypnosis can she recall her marriage to Richard Crane and the nightmare they encountered leading to the gruesome death of her husband in the Bayou. By the movie's end the doctors decide it is best that her past life remain forgotten.

Richard Crane's character, that of a former military flyer who broke every bone in his body from a horrible plane crash, received experimental treatments at his mother's plantation deep in Louisiana swamp country. However, while on a train honeymooning with Garland, Crane receives a wire with such bad news (he is losing his human identity) that he immediately abandons his wife and leaves the train at its first available stop. The wily and deeply in love Garland traces him to his home and faces horror she never imagined.

First of all, we are treated to an over-the-top but juicy Lon Chaney, Jr. supporting characterization as a Bayou bumpkin who lost one hand to the "slimy gators," and is now forced to wear a hook. His hatred for the alligators seems secondary to the passion he feels for the sensual Garland, whose face he lustfully rubs with his steel hook. Pretty soon Chaney, Jr. is preying upon both the gators he loves to run over in his truck or shoot in penny arcade fashion every night and the non-interested Garland. Chaney, Jr.'s performance is too broad and overall ridiculous, yet it is definitely a memorable performance that children fondly remember.

Richard Crane probably submits the performance of his career here, as the brooding and frightened macho husband who cannot share his personal swamp demons with his new wife. At the plantation Crane's character is still human, although his face and arms have taken on the roughness of alligator skin as his treatments are turning him into something quasi-human. Crane, fearing for his humanity, forces scientist George Macready to use the full dose of his radiation treatments to either cure or kill him, but Chaney, Jr.'s interference (and striking death by electrocution caused by his metal hook touching an electrical apparatus in the lab) causes the house to explode... but not before Crane is transformed into an actual were-gator whose former soft skin becomes alligator tough and his face and head erupt into a large alligator snoot. The makeup is pure rubber suit and looks it; however, the actual makeup concept is pretty imaginative for a 1959 B programmer. Within minutes of wife Beverly Garland seeing her husband's transformation and screaming her head off, the Crane gator walks into quicksand and submerges far too quickly.

*The Alligator People*, a favorite of mine as a kid, features stark mood, fog-shrouded set design and haunting CinemaScope photography. The performances, mostly by tried and true veterans, are more than effective, and the monster makeup delivers the goods. The film's only flaw is a too leisurely pace with the need for one or two additional shocking pay-off sequences. But for a late 1950s matinee romp, *The Alligator People* entertains.

**Dead and Buried**
Movie: 3.0; Disc: 3.5
[Blue Underground]

Now the horrible truth can be told... the decade of the 1980s was the worst decade in the history of the horror film. After a resurgence of gruesome independently produced American horrors and the proliferation of Eurohorror, the 1980s saw Hollywood bankrupt with innovations and rehashing imitation. Copycat movies resulted... with a few exceptions.

*Dead and Buried*, script credited to Ronald Shuster and Dan O'Bannon, directed by Gary Sherman (*Raw Meat*), is an exception and remains one of the best independently produced horror movies of the 1980s.

First, what *Dead and Buried* does right is create an air of mystery and horror that draws the viewer immediately into the movie. We are confronted with the small rural town of Potter's Bluff (an allusion to *It's A Wonderful Life*'s alternate universe if mean Mr. Potter took over and controlled the town), a small community of seemingly friendly people, the type of town where everyone knows one another. In the film's first sequence a vacationing photographer meets a beautiful blonde on the beach, and in her naïve sexually charged way, she immediately starts to pose and even undress for him. Then purring, "Do you want me?" she begins to nuzzle close to the beaming man. Suddenly a crowd descends upon the poor sap, kicking and beating him over the head and finally wrapping him in fish net against a pole. "Welcome to Potter's Bluff," one man announces, pouring gasoline over him and setting him ablaze. The entire assembled crowd stands by smiling, watching him burn to death. This same scenario is repeated shortly thereafter with a drunken homeless person who is harpooned and stabbed, as the wild-eyed mob snaps photos and giggles as the poor victim suffers and dies. This mob is visceral yet engaging.

Our titular hero, the town sheriff (James Fermenting), a man who earned a master's degree in criminology but decided to serve his home town, is mystified by these horrible, mutilating crimes. The beach victim, found at the wheel of an overturned auto accident, is burned to a crisp, yet his jaw drops and a chilling scream emulates from his throat. This victim is about to be questioned by the police, his head and body bandaged, when his nurse, the same seductive blonde from the beach, sticks a long hypodermic needle into his eye, instantly killing him. Strangely, days later the man is perfectly healed and working at the local service station.

The sheriff's investigation involves the local eccentric and nattily dressed town undertaker, Jack Albertson, who brags of his artistry and the fact that a closed coffin spells defeat for him. Albertson, always energetic and dancing to 1930s pop music as he works, seems to be disguising a sinister underbelly.

Soon the sheriff discovers his wife hiding a strange book on witchcraft and voodooism. Then a family of three stop at the town diner asking for directions, soon to experience a car accident which causes them to take refuge in an old house without electricity and covered with cobwebs (why then does the father venture alone down into the cellar with the

happy wife yelling, is anyone home?). Shadows loom outside the windows. When our familiar town mob (now we begin to recognize that members of the murderous mob hold down regular jobs in the community) breaks through the glass and attempts to murder the family, somehow they escape in a chilling visual sequence involving spooky, shadowy cinematography and well-executed editing. The next day their smashed car is pulled out of the river and the little boy turns up in a school classroom, just a quick flash among his classmates telegraphing the fact that this boy was apparently dead but is now alive.

While the film's sense of dread and mystery is quite successful, the film's reliance on gore effects, created by the master Stan Winston no less, tend to go unnecessarily too far and shots of rocks crushing skulls, people burned alive and victims who get needles in the eye seem excessive. The film's final surprise, that this is a town of living corpses, people who died, reconstructed by masterful Jack Albertson and ultimately reanimated (although still dead and decaying) is a shocking one. In the film's final moments the sheriff learns his wife

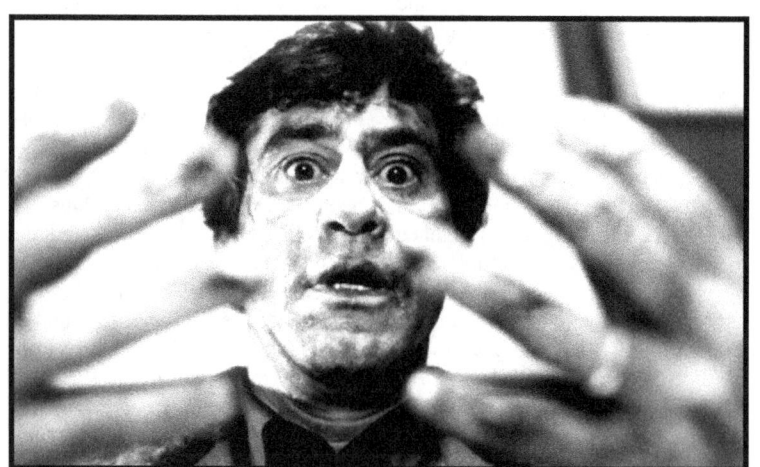

murdered him, shown via home movies no less, while having sex. He was stabbed repeatedly in the back. Looking now at his decaying fingers, the tender voice of Albertson states, let me fix that up, as the film ends on a freeze frame.

*Dead and Buried* succeeds on the strength of its quirky and well-executed performances (especially Jack Albertson's) and its mystery-dominated horror plot that keeps the audience guessing right up until the ending. Stan Winston's makeup contributions are brilliant, especially a mortuary sequence where the smashed face of a teenage girl is restored to its original beauty, the final touch of adding an artificial eye to the socket a grisly coda. But instead of simply cutting away at this point, the girl's eyes open and she sits up and gets off the slab. Surprises like this abound, and the discrepancy between the Andy of Mayberry good people of Potter's Bluff and the insane mob of murderers that they sometimes become mesmerizes the audience and keeps it on its toes.

This Blue Underground two-disc set contains a pristine print of the movie and adds a second disc of extras (three audio commentaries, multiple documentaries, still and poster gallery) for the consummate fan of the movie. While the 1980s produced mostly cookie-cutter movies, thank heavens movies such as *Dead and Buried* existed as well.

**Cursed [Unrated Version]**
Movie: 3.0; Disc: 3.5
[Dimension]

It may be true that horror auteurs Tobe Hooper, Wes Craven and John Carpenter never lived up to their potential 30 years after, but Wes Craven's *Cursed*, scripted by Kevin Williamson, is a fantastic mainstream popcorn horror movie... but then again Williamson and Carpenter blew it with two pivotal miscalculations that undermine the entire production.

But first, what makes *Cursed* classic Craven? First of all, the casting of Christina Ricci was utter perfection, as Ricci is quirky, oddly sexual and quite talented. She is not conventionally sensual but her performances always manage to sizzle and yet be totally honest. For instance, one brief eccentric sequence in her office demonstrates her talent when a strange scent catches her nose and she decides to explore to find out its source. Literally prowling down office alleyways, wiggling her hips and literally sniffing out co-workers, she finally sashays into the ladies' lavatory and finds a woman bent over the sink with a nosebleed. Ricci takes what might have been bland on paper into something oddball and wonderful. Fortunately, a youthful cast of characters surrounds her, delivering the goods, and offers her effective character support. As with Craven's finest films, the disintegrating nuclear family becomes the focus, with a parentless household of young sister and brother holding itself together fueling the dramatic tension.

Second, the makeup effects of the werewolf, both mechanical suit and CGI, are very frightening, and Craven wisely chooses to show his beast during the initial sequence only sporadically... the werewolf standing on hind legs viewed from a victim's perspective looking out from beneath a car, a flash of fur here, an eye and face quick cut there. Such quick editing makes the werewolf truly frightening.

Third, the major werewolf sequences are classic in execution. We have the car crash where the Ricci character Ellie and her younger brother collide with a car driven by Shannon Elizabeth, who was warned earlier in the night by Gypsy Portia de Rossi to beware the beast. As Ricci and Jesse Eisenberg crawl through the wreckage of the overturned vehicle, Elizabeth hanging upside down until her rescuers can undo her seat belt, we expect to see the wolf attack from the rear. Noises emanate from behind the rescuers and they fearfully look back over their shoulders. However, the wolf attacks by breaking auto glass and coming for Elizabeth in front, dragging her out of the car and through the woods. Craven's style—expecting an attack from the rear but having one from the front—shines here. Moments later, Elizabeth's body is flung through the air at Ricci, and when the body lands with a thud, audiences (in the unrated version) can see the lower half of her body is missing. Overkill, yes, but the scene is very effective. Just as effective is the parking garage attack where the lovely Mya character is pursued by the beast to the elevator, where the feisty teen battles for her life. The elevator stops between floors, but the hole is too small for the werewolf to squeeze through so it backs off. Mya sees the garage door leading up to the second floor flapping, meaning the werewolf figures out she will start the elevator and exit on the next floor. The race is on and the tension is riveting. Unfortunately, the werewolf arrives first, smashes in the metal doors and devours the little lovely before she can escape. But once again effective acting, cinematography and editing make this sequence a classic one. And we even have two more sequences that are just as effective.

So, where are the two major misfires? First of all, Ellie's (Ricci) brooding boyfriend Jake (Joshua Jackson) turns out to be a werewolf, but seemingly a sympathetic one. He tells the bitten Ellie that he can protect her from the curse. He is the Bryonic hero and plays his part to the hilt. In the film's final sequence he mentions that Ellie can only be free by killing him, but the totally sympathetic teen wolf suddenly announces he will kill Ellie's brother so the two of them can be free. Jesse Eisenberg, who has created a very warm nerd-strikes-back character, starts to crawl on the ceiling, reminding viewers that Wes Craven pulled similar stunts from his early *Nightmare on Elm Street* movies. And while Craven directs this final confrontation to perfection, it is Kevin Williamson's script that attempts to solve the dilemma of brother and sister werewolves in too pat a manner by having Jake announce the far too mechanical and totally unsatisfying ending. Since Jake has been sympathetic, he now has to turn evil to allow the innocent brother and sister to save their own lives by taking his. The script rings false here.

And the second major misfire is again caused by Williamson's script, but here director Craven is just as guilty. In the climax at the horror wax museum (which houses a magnificent likeness of Lon Chaney, Jr. as the Wolf Man), the evil werewolf is revealed to be Ellie's snotty assistant Joanie (Judy Greer) from work, and when the police arrive, werewolf Joanie is hiding in the balcony above. Ellie, resorting to playing a clever trick, describes Joanie for the police as having a bony ass and fat thighs. Suddenly the vain werewolf makes its dramatic appearance simply to give Joanie the finger. Clever yes, and a great visual gag, agreed. However, the *tone* of the film is compromised here. What has been a totally frightening and serious horror drama (with humor wisely used as an extension of character) sinks to the lowest common denominator and uncomfortably morphs into another teen comedy lark, if only for a moment. *Cursed* loses its ground here and the sudden shift in tone destroys everything the film worked so hard to create. The furry "finger" seems totally out of place. I should mention also the family dog's transformation into were-dog, and while the mayhem the pet causes is tense, the sequence again seems out of place and silly.

So *Cursed* again demonstrates what happens when gifted filmmakers resort to sloppy script writing, demographics-targeted audiences and sacrificing well-crafted performances and mood to kowtow to adolescent lowbrow sensibilities. *Cursed* has all the potential to be among the best of Wes Craven's horror pictures, but these two major misfires reduce the film to being merely a good one with a few standout sequences and a solid performance by Christina Ricci.

Extras include documentaries and selected sequences with audio commentary. The pristine print (deep blacks and intense colors zipping off the screen) and Dolby 5.1 soundtrack make this DVD a showcase one to demonstrate your A/V system to friends.

**Dark Water**
Movie: 3.0; Disc: 3.0
[ADV]

From *Ringu*'s director (Hideo Nakata), based on another story by *Ringu*'s Soji Suzuki, comes *Dark Water* (2002), another terrifying vision of ghosts and sacrifice. Once again American producers dipped from the Japanese well when the American version starring Jennifer Connolly was released last year.

And once again the original production demonstrates why Japan lies at the cutting edge of horror films this decade. To be honest, *Dark Water* is less successful than *Ju-On* and *Ringu*, yet it is vastly superior to most contemporary horror chillers. The film's strength is its murky, moody photography, its blistering editing, its emphasis on acting and characterization and its slow building sense of dread and horror.

Recently separated mother Yoshimi (Hitomi Kuroki), fighting an intense custody battle over her six-year-old daughter Ikuko (Rio Kanno), is forced to move with her child into a very old apartment building which is gloomy and in terrible need of maintenance, with water drips and puddles

everywhere. The manager who shows the apartment glances upward to grimace at the increasing wet spot on the ceiling and hopes Yoshimi does not see it.

Her ruthless husband tries to show that Yoshimi cannot properly care for the child, when she takes on a new job as editor in a very undesirable office where she often has to work late, leaving the daughter to stand outside her school. The father becomes upset when he arrives to pick up the child from school who is alone, waiting on the parking lot and vulnerable from any sexual predator.

Soon both mother and child have visions of a water-soaked child, about the same age as Ikuko, who seems to be living in the apartment immediately above their own (and must be the source of all the water drippings). The child and its water-soaked squeaking shoes appear when Ikuko plays hide-and-seek at school and the child's little red bag is abandoned on the rooftop of the apartment.

Yoshimi discovers that years ago the child fell into a water filtration tank on the apartment's roof and drowned (shades of *Ringu* I know), thus the motivation for all the horrific water imagery. Ikuko runs bath water one night after tufts of hair come out of the faucet while she gets a glass of water. The bath water is dark and murky and bubbles. As the water overflows Ikuko tries in vain to shut off the valves but the water keeps surging. Soon the arms of the ghost child emerge from the water and grasp Ikuko and try to pull her in. Yoshimi arrives home and finds her child wet and unconscious on the floor. Yoshimi cradles the broken child and carries her to the elevator hitting the up button. Immediately the elevator fills with dripping, leaky water and the electrical wiring shorts out stopping the elevator at the next floor up. While stuck, Yoshimi watches as Ikuko emerges from an open apartment dazed and wet. But who is the child the mother cradles in her arms? In an abrupt shock, a decaying and faceless child lunges toward its mother figure and clutches her as Ikuko approaches the elevator and watches mother and child, still in the elevator, start to move upward. Ikuko faces the door and waits for the elevator to open, which it does, spilling out tons of water upon her, knocking her down. But no people are inside. Her mother and the ghost child are gone, and Ikuko lies wet and abandoned. The wide-eyed puzzlement on the child's face and Yoshimi's haunted resolve to protect her daughter linger long.

A coda occurs 10 years later that reunites 16-year-old Ikuko and her mother in a tender but haunting finale… with the presence of the ghost child always lingering in the background, unseen by Ikuko.

The problem with *Dark Water* is the simple fact that too much of the movie is devoted to parental divorce, angst and the problems every single mother faces alone. The film takes too long to generate its supernatural elements and introduce the ghost. *Dark Water* just cannot make up its mind if it wants to be dysfunctional drama or a horror movie, but once the horror elements are introduced, they become emotionally stronger because of the family elements. *Dark Water* is no *Ringu* or *Ju-On*, but it is an imaginative and terrifying exercise in ghosts and horror. The DVD is available with an American 5.1 surround sound and a Japanese version with English dubbing. A theatrical trailer is included.

### Rabid
Movie: 2.5; Disc: 3.5
[Somerville House]

Disappointingly, David Cronenberg's first two mainstream features, *Shivers* and *Rabid*, do not hold up well. Films that seemed so innovative and terrifying back in the mid-1970s seem almost clichéd today.

*Rabid*, released in 1977, stars adult film star Marilyn Chambers as the sexy plague bearer. Just as she demonstrated in her porno movies, Chambers can be the innocent girl next door one moment and a sexual predator the next. Not surprisingly, Marilyn Chambers' performance is most effective playing the victim of a terrible motorcycle accident who receives cutting edge surgery at the Kiloid Clinic. Doctors there produce a disease-bearing vagina in her armpit with a bloody phallus parasite that emerges to inject itself into victims and both drain their blood and infect them with a variation of a new rabies virus. Within six hours the infected ones become zombies, foam at the mouth and bite any human being within reach. Thus the plague is spread, not unlike the premise of *Shivers* (which was limited by budget to a high-rise apartment building). *Rabid* has a larger budget and the mayhem does spread outside the clinic, yet the film seems like another case of deja-vu and is too much a retread of the *Shivers* themes.

David Cronenberg's direction is still intense and he is able to build chills most subtly. For instance, in one sequence a sexy brunette is lying half sprawled, legs spread, wearing a bathing suit in a hot tub. Rose (Chambers), wearing something flimsy, asks if she can join her in the tub, saying that her body is achy from being in the hospital bed recovering for so long. Immediately the brunette registers fear and unease and makes an excuse to exit, but the demure Chambers purrs for her to please remain so she can chat. Within moments Chambers, an innocent and weary smile on her lips, approaches the brunette and without warning grabs her in a death hug and feeds while the woman struggles. Sequences like these demonstrate the visceral power of Cronenberg's cinema, but too much of the movie shows infected madmen biting innocent victims and the film seems to be a George Romero clone. But then Cronenberg delivers the ultimate shock scene, quite fascinating, as a walk-in freezer door is opened at the clinic to reveal the dead and frozen body of a beautiful blonde, her frozen hands laying atop bare legs that seem to connect Cronenberg's chief imagery of sexuality and death. The clothed woman, her face distorted and grimacing, is somehow fascinating to behold and becomes a dominant image that lingers. Cronenberg's visual eyes always manage to create such stark images (this image used quite effectively on the film's poster) that would probably be ignored if handled by anyone else.

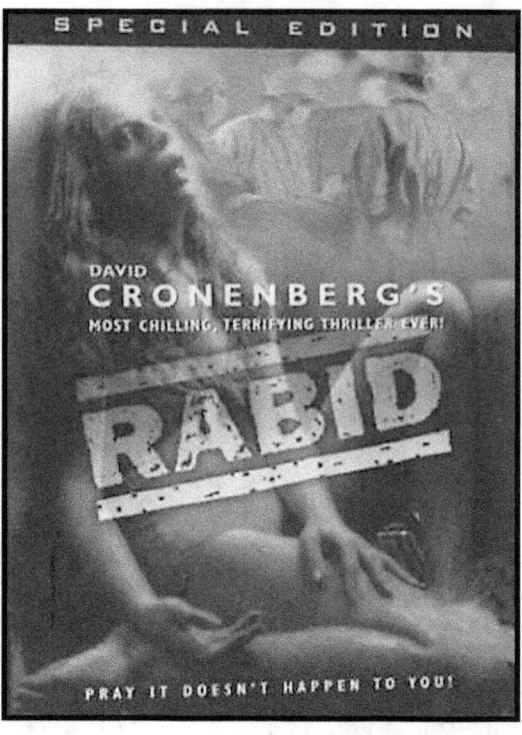

The movie's ending is very disappointing, the Rose character allowing herself to be victimized by an infected male, and within hours she too lies comatose, then dead, and finally she is literally picked up by the haz-mat team (dressed in protective garments) who casually lift and dispose of her in the back of a garbage truck along with bags and other trash. The credits come up. The sequence is too reminiscent of George Romero's end to *Night of the Living Dead* where rescue teams dispose of zombies in such methodical ways. The ending seems unsatisfying, as though the plague has played itself out and only the disposal of the infected corpses remains. Absolutely no drama exists to show the satisfaction of defeating the plague; instead, the movie ends when Rose ends.

Besides featuring a good print (it's not anamorphic nor has it been enhanced for 16:9 monitors), the DVD features audio commentary by David Cronenberg and also features an on-air interview with the director/writer. Trailers, bios, photo and poster galleries are included.

### New York Ripper
Movie 2.5; Disc: 3.5
[Anchor Bay]

Lucio Fulci's films include his masterworks *The Beyond* and *Zombie*; however, the second tier offers movies such as *New York Ripper*, one of his movies that mines the same creative territory as the giallo of Dario Argento.

Amazing, for a country that is the heart of the Roman Catholic Church with its traditional second- class citizenship for women (they are unable to become priests, they are unable to practice birth control and they are unable to have a choice in the matter of abortions), auteurs like Argento and Fulci built a cinematic career based in part around the theme of misogyny with beautiful women, sometimes nude, dismembered, tortured and viciously attacked and often murdered.

Dario Argento has a unique visual style, often ethereal and dreamlike, his stylized violence artistically rendered with finesse. Lucio Fulci is more the butcher with brutality and sudden shock substituting for visual style. Take the opening of *New York Ripper*, for example. Here a leggy young beauty riding a motorbike looks for her former boyfriend's car where she passionately uses her lipstick to write "SHIT" on the front windshield. The women, in a setting similar to an urban underground parking garage, is confronted by a man who quacks like a duck. Soon she is attacked by this fiend who pulls her back inside the car when she tries to escape, his sharp silver blade poised and held in dramatic stance ready to strike. Most of the slashings penetrate her chest and breasts, but he slits her torso from below her belly button up toward her breast, her mouth and face writhing in pain as she screams out in anguish for the final seconds of her life. While the torso-slitting effects are less than convincing, the camera takes its time showing the torture and ritualistic slaying as something that spectators are supposed to linger on. The entire sequence panders to viewers who enjoy seeing a sexy woman tortured and murdered. In the following sequence we see this same woman naked and dead on a metallic slab, the horrible slashings on her well-rounded breasts having been sewed back together in death.

The movie features about four or five such sequences showing females (and in one case a male) tortured, slashed and made to die slowly as the camera lovingly lingers. Even for the 1980s, Fulci's technically ritualistic murders were disturbing and went further than similar American-made movies.

While this Italian film had exteriors filmed in New York City, most of the interiors were filmed in Italy and the American dubbing is ridiculous, with voice actors accentuating a Brooklyn accent or overstating American dialects and voice inflections. Even the attitudes, clothing and interaction between actors become one long stereotype of America. To me it was very funny but also distracting by virtue of being more than slightly over the top.

To Fulci's credit, the script and the suspense generated in the events leading up to the slayings is rendered effectively. We have terrifying sequences of the duck-voiced fiend babbling over the phone to the police, approaching his victim and luring unsuspecting women to their doom. The use of the fiend's duck voice and quacking sounds might seem silly and counter to the horrific mood, but for some strange reason the psycho's duck leanings only make him more terrifying and frightening. Once he strikes, using a razor blade to slowly slice flesh or cut an exposed nipple, or even cut into an open eyeball (Fulci's calling card from *Zombie*), the visuals go overboard and seem once again to relish the torture of women. I won't condone those sequences. But the immediate tension and fear generated leading up to those sequences of mayhem are often well done.

While *The New York Ripper* appears to be second-rate Argento that seems more akin to a lesson in butchery than artistically rendered movie-making, Lucio Fulci's direction is often sharp and visually based. He lacks the artistic style of a Bava or Argento, but the Italian director tries hard to craft a tale of a city haunted by a duck-quacking serial killer. While the film ultimately fails and pales alongside the much superior *The Beyond*, the film contains a few moments of effectively generated horror.

For extras, the disc contains a bio of Lucio Fulci and a theatrical trailer.

**The Exorcist: The Beginning**
Movie: 3.0; Disc: 3.5
[Warner]

One of the essential improvements of the Millennium horror movie, something that doomed the 1980s and most of the 1990s, is the establishment of serious tone in horror once again. Yes, we still have horror films with wisecracking teens and one-liner villains acting as though they were at open mike night. But movies like Renny Harlin's *The Exorcist: The Beginning* are deadly serious, with well-drawn characters and an intriguing plot that attempts to make the audience think. Even though *The Beginning* does not cut any new ground, it is a thoroughly entertaining character-based horror thriller (and while the CGI effects are used, they are kept to a minimum and do compromise the production).

Everyone knows by this time that director Paul Schrader first made his version of this movie (called *Dominion*), which was shelved after being deemed too arty and lacking enough blood and gore for the investors. Then Renny Harlin was hired to re-shoot the entire production after making changes that met studio/production demands.

Harlin's film both begins and ends with a sweeping human massacre, the opening battle occurring 1500 years ago with armies of soldiers crucified upside down and writhing on their wooden crosses, the carnage filling an entire battlefield. Truly the sight of such human suffering is an image that lingers long in the viewer's mind. And at the conclusion, another massacre occurs, this time the tragedy half-buried by an African desert sand storm that hides most of the corpses.

The movie focuses on the personal battle of faith fought by Father Merrin (Stellan Skarsgard), in this prelude to the original *The Exorcist*, which features an elderly Merrin exorcising the demon from innocent preteen Regan. It seems the good priest gave up the priesthood after World War II when he was forced to pick innocent citizens to be executed (10 of them) or else everyone would be slaughtered, including children. "God is not here today, Priest" is the mantra constantly repeated throughout the movie. Shocked and shamed by such human atrocities, Merrin returns to archaeology and becomes a mercenary hired to bring back a statue of an ancient demon Pazuzu (the demon from the original film). Merrin journeys to Kenya to join the crew unearthing a Christian Byzantine church buried and built overtop an ancient Pagan temple created to honor Pazuzu. The most obvious question is why has a Christian church been built over a Pagan one, and why was the Christian church supposedly buried upon its completion? Of course this is the location of the film's opening mas-

sacre sequence, stated by one young priest as being the spot on Earth where Lucifer landed when God expelled him from Heaven. The film nicely establishes the church and surroundings as a place of all-consuming evil.

Soon mayhem and bloodshed reach both the tribal village and the expedition dig camp. A butterfly collector sees his mounted specimens flutter and come to life, a butterfly emerging from his mouth, into which the man inserts the barrel of his revolver and fires. In another sequence, the original archaeologist of the dig, now confined to a mental asylum, cuts his body and throat as Merrin enters his room to question him. A cute little tribal boy, Joseph (Remy Sweeney), seems to be possessed by the demon, and when horrible things happen, he simply goes into either a trance or has a seizure. In another

effective sequence, an annoying monkey suddenly transforms into a hyena and then a pack of them attack in the darkness to literally chew a victim apart.

Of course children and possession is exactly what the viewer expects with any sequel to *The Exorcist*, and that's where the screenplay by William Peter Blatty (based upon the original story by William Wisher, Jr.) shines. For the entire bulk of the movie, audiences simply accept that Joseph is possessed by demon Pazuzu, but during the film's conclusion viewers discover Pazuzu actually possesses another human and only makes it seem the little tribal boy was touched by evil in order to fuel a rebellion that would bring British imperialists and the native tribe to bloody warfare, reflecting what happened 1500 years ago.

*The Exorcist: The Beginning* features many marvelous sequences, all of them chilling and well executed. Already mentioned was the CGI-fueled hyena massacre. We also have a sensual yet frightening sequence when the doctor, Sarah, undresses and showers, the generator lights flickering and going out, as the female, dripping and wrapped scantily in a towel, explores her living area hearing strange noises. Suddenly, and shockingly, the lights flash back on and blaring music startles the audience. Then, to add a second shock, Sarah looks back and sees bloody footprints and drops of blood peppering the floor.

She glances downward and sees the lower portion of her towel bathed in menstrual blood. Very odd and unsettling, one climax ups the ante on the other. The tribal ritualistic sacrifice of young Joseph, already mentioned, is punctuated by chanting and the entire sequence is juxtaposed to the chilling sequence where Merrin decides to dig up tribal graves that have never been explained. So the camera cuts back and forth between the frantic shoveling in the dark and the grotesquely painted warriors raising a dagger above Joseph's prostrate body. Such a sequence, carefully orchestrated and punctuated with music, sounds, chants and dancing, creates a stellar horror rush.

But the film's payoff comes when Merrin prays to regain his faith so he can carry out his exorcism of Pazuzu, with innocent Joseph by his side, underground, in the temple of Pazuzu, the fiend trying to seduce the priest while engaging in a battle to the death. In a sense this climactic sequence lacks the subtlety and style of the earlier moneymaker scenes, but the CGI-enhanced shots of the demon writhing and scaling the temple walls is horrific and unsettling. In another shot the demon comes running full speed in the semi-darkness down a long tunnel toward Merrin. But, of course, what good is an *Exorcist* sequel without a profane exorcism?

By the final shot, Merrin has donned his white collar and become Father Merrin once again, and the film's intense character study of Merrin makes Stellan Skarsgard an actor to watch (although the long and angular Max Van Sydow and the stockier, puffier Skarsgard do not appear to be the same person, a minor quibble). *The Exorcist: The Beginning* is an effective, straightforward and intense exercise in visual horror and it makes me want to see Paul Schrader's original version.

### Trauma
Movie: 3.0; Disc: 3.5
[Anchor Bay]

Since William Lustig left Anchor Bay to form Blue Underground, Anchor Bay has been generally coasting on its laurels, as far as horror exclusives go. However, Anchor Bay is back in the saddle with deluxe (and affordably priced) versions of two Dario Argento movies, *Trauma* (1993) and *The Card Player* (2003). *Trauma*, considered by some to be Argento's last great film, following *Opera* and *Phenomena* by several years, is marketed as "fully restored and totally uncut for the first time ever in America!"

*Trauma* returns Argento to his giallo roots and the movie is a success, even if not one of Argento's better movies. For the first time Argento filmed entirely in the United States, in Minneapolis no less, so the movie contains an English soundtrack. The music score by Pino Donaggio is disappointing and fails to evoke even one-tenth the mood of any of his Bernard Herrmann-esque scores for Brian De Palma. The cinematography by Raffaele Mertes is stark and hard-hitting, often relaying upon subjective points of view for the horror effect. Tom Savini creates the special makeup effects for the first time in an Argento production and does a good job.

The most interesting aspect of the production is the up-and-coming Asia Argento, Dario's daughter, in the starring role, that of anorexic 16-year-old Aura who escapes from an asylum and avoids living with her affluent mother Piper Laurie. Befriended by former junkie David (Christopher Rydell, son of director Mark), Aura warms to the kindred spirit and soon is living with him (platonically).

In such Argento-land surroundings, we encounter the Headhunter serial killer, who only murders during rainstorms and uses a steel wire motorized saw to decapitate his victims. The mood is set in the film's opening slaying when an unseen chiropractic patient arrives after business hours to receive back adjustment treatment, the rain pouring outside the window. As the black chiropractor turns around to get some papers, the patient whips out a hammer and knocks the woman senseless, semi-conscious, but she's unable to move. The steel wire is wrapped around her neck, and within moments, the buzz intensifies as the wire cuts cleanly through her neck. Of course the head becomes the killer's trophy.

Aura becomes involved when her mother and father both appear to be victims of the serial killer, and after Aura and David investigate further, it seems all the murder victims knew one another and have been involved together in a medical scandal of some type. Also Dr. Judd (Frederic Forrest), the nut case psychiatrist who heads the mental clinic to which Aura had been confined, seems to be suspicious and somehow involved in the medical scandal, perhaps even as the serial killer himself.

Yes, the plot does become rather complex and over-blown, especially when the killer beheads a nurse inside a hospital, setting off the sprinkler system to create the rain he needs in order to do his dirty work. But in a wonderfully eerie follow-up scene, David arrives at the murder scene seconds after the decapitation and attempts to speak to and listen to the severed head, eyes and mouth open, bleeding all over the floor. So while Argento's story gets carried away with itself, the director's style remains horrific and mesmerizing, both at the same time.

Asia Argento, claiming she really starved herself to play the role, looks haunting and haunted, bony and angular, but always exotic with those piercing eyes and dark features. In one odd sequence, at David's place, Argento undresses and takes off her bra, exposing herself as David watches silently. Instead of looking alluring, Aura appears to be uncomfortable and quickly covers up and turns away. This sense of hiding some deep secret, of being controlled by her eating disorder, makes her performance unsettling and real. In an earlier scene set in a dinner, David implores Aura to eat, and when she takes a nibble or two, the camera follows her rushing to the bathroom to vomit up the food. So the performance becomes riveting, Asia Argento playing a victim of an eating disorder, and also playing another victim of her dominant mother.

Again, *Trauma* is not one of Argento's best works, yet, at the same time, it is always challenging and visually stylish. Frederic Forrest's performance is oddly quirky and the usually eccentric Brad Dourif is rather intense but almost pretty-boy ordinary. So again Argento likes to mix things up a tad and play against stereotypes. The rainy-at-night sequence of Asia running in back of her mother's house into the woods, to see the split second image of what she believes to be her mother beheaded, is a classic horror nightmare put to film.

The abundant extras on this DVD include a documentary, *Love, Death and Trauma*, including onscreen interviews with Dario Argento. An audio commentary comes from author Alan Jones. Tom Savini's making-of documentary appears, deleted scenes, still and poster gallery, theatrical trailer and Argento biography follow also. It is a nice package highlighting a beautifully rendered 16:9 enhanced anamorphic print of the movie. When thinking of horror movies made in 1993, surely *Trauma* must earn a few extra points for rising above much of the mediocrity of the times.

**The Card Player**
Movie: 3.0; Disc: 3.5
[Anchor Bay]

Dario Argento, generally considered to be off his game since the early 1990s, demonstrated recently in 2003 that his instincts and visual skills as a director are still intact. No one will ever put *The Card Player* in the same category as *Suspiria* or *Deep Red,* but *The Card Player* is an excellent serial killer suspense thriller that uses all of Argento's primary strengths. It is an Argento movie that for once offers effective acting. Stefania Rocca portrays a female police detective and Liam Cunningham (of *Dog Soldiers*) portrays a heavy-drinking Irish policeman reduced to working missing persons in England because he shot and killed an under-aged criminal suspect.

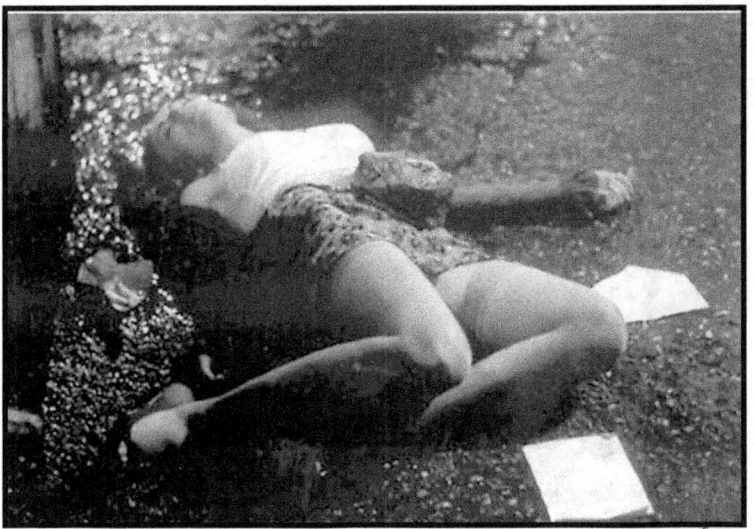

*The Card Player* is the most recent Argento production, and it definitely bodes well for Argento's creative future. The plot is fairly basic. A serial killer who plays video poker notifies the local police that they must play five games of poker to save the life of a young female victim (her tortured face with mouth taped shut screams and writhes and a web camcorder records her torture, all in close up). Either the girl will be set free (if the police win) or continually tortured and ultimately murdered (if the serial killer wins). However, for each individual game the police lose, the girl will lose a body part. At first the police commissioner refuses to indulge the perverse cravings of such a diseased mind, and by the next day or so the kidnap victim is found nude, in the river, decaying and showing signs of mutilation. In a rather odd autopsy scene, an Italian Danny DeVito clone merrily dances and sings as he displays the girl's body and allows the Liam Cunningham character to literally probe the corpse, pulling seed pods out of orifices. Interestingly enough, the corpse looks like a corpse with horrifying frozen features and discolored skin. It's not just another pretty nude on the slab.

Soon the police play against the so-called "card player" and lose, resulting in another corpse being washed up on shore. Getting smart, the police enlist the help of an obsessive video poker player who is very skilled and knows the strategy of playing the game. However, even though he is winning in his game, the female victim struggles and frees herself, only to be butchered by the fiend, who attacks her with his knife. Although the police were winning the series, the victim's attempted escape negates the card game and the rules change. However, when the commissioner's daughter (Fiore Argento, Dario's other daughter) is kidnapped, the video poker champion wins three straight games and the daughter is released unharmed. The serial killer does have a sense of honor and he plays fair. However, for revenge, he pays a beautiful woman to lure the young card player to the docks when she is suddenly shot and killed. A robotic voice then orders the man to enter one of two doors ahead (one will lead to freedom, the other to his death). Of course Argento's visual power is back. Once the man runs inside one of the doors, he is caught in a rat's maze of twisted, dark corridors that seem to lead only into darker and scarier territory. A rope is dropped over the man's head and a powerboat drags him into dark, terrifying waters. The man soon cuts the rope and bobs and weaves in the water, smiling all the time. The man feels he has beaten the card player but he fails to see the quiet boat sneak up behind him, and before his smile becomes a frown, an unknown assailant appears with a metal hook that rips into the unsuspecting man's neck, killing him almost immediately. The police suddenly lose their ace in the hole.

During the film's gripping climax, policewoman Stefania Rocco confronts the killer and the two of them, chained to train tracks, play five games of poker to decide who will get the key to unlock the chains to escape the speeding train. And the outcome is not as predictable as movie viewers might assume. In one visually dazzling sequence, the person hit by the train tumbles beneath the cars bouncing up and down over the tracks in a horrifying death scene that Argento simply excels at creating.

*The Card Player* does not introduce any new Argento themes (we have graphic female death scenes, intense stalkings down dank corridors, frustrated police, an isolated country estate that overflows with floating white buds, surprising character revelations, etc.), yet the movie is not simply rehash either. *The Card Player* demonstrates Argento's refinement of style and becomes a re-defining of older themes. The print used here is pristine and the musical score by former Goblin member Claudio Simonetti is a return to form and is quite excellent. Extras include audio commentary, a documentary featuring Dario Argento and another featuring Claudio Simonetti. We also have an Argento bio, theatrical trailer, behind the scenes footage and the electronic press kit.

Anchor Bay has done a great service to horror film fans by presenting these two Dario Argento movies uncut, pristine and so well packaged with so many interesting bonus features. For those who doubted the long-lasting appeal of the Italian master of horror, now is the time for another evaluation.

**The Ring Two (Unrated Edition)**
Movie: 3.0; Disc: 3.5
[Dreamworks]

Director Hideo Nakata created *Ringu* and *Ringu 2*. Then the American version of *The Ring* followed, directed by Gore Verbinski. For the sequel, *The Ring Two*, the production ran into trouble and the Japanese originator Hideo Nakata replaced the original director.

The bottom line is that *The Ring Two* is not as successful as the original, but it still becomes a horror film of merit. Thank heavens the Japanese influx of horror to American shores upped the scare quotient. The Japanese depend less on gore and special effects and more on directorial manipulation that creeps out audiences and truly gets under our skin.

Within 15 minutes the movie does away with its videotape urban legend premise left over from the original film (a male teen has an hour remaining before he is destroyed by the watching-the-video curse, but he tries to snare an innocent female to watch the video to doom her and save his life). From this point onward Naomi Watts as mother Rachel works overtime to save her son Aidan (David Dorfman) from being possessed by evil Samara (Kelly Stables). Although dead, Samara just wants to find a mother who loves her. And by possessing her son, Aidan, Samara can be part of a loving family.

Audiences can criticize the lack of a developed plot, but the movie comprises sequences showing subtle ways in which Aidan comes under the influence of Samara (calling his mother Rachel, not mommy). Once again the movie is filled with water imagery and the exploding bathtub with water running toward the ceiling becomes a major sequence, with shell-shocked Aidan being pulled beneath the dark bath waters as Samara emerges.

Unfortunately, the climax involves Rachel being transported via a fancy special effects sequence to the well where Samara died, becoming a tad overblown, with Rachel's escape trying to climb up the well's walls being pursued by creepily flexible Samara, who moves in a terrifyingly herky-jerky fashion (in this sequence Samara is played by a contortionist). The scene's only false moment is when Rachel escapes and seals the well shut, cursing out Samara in a rather insensitive and heartless manner. This sequence might be a crowd pleaser, but it's emotionally hollow.

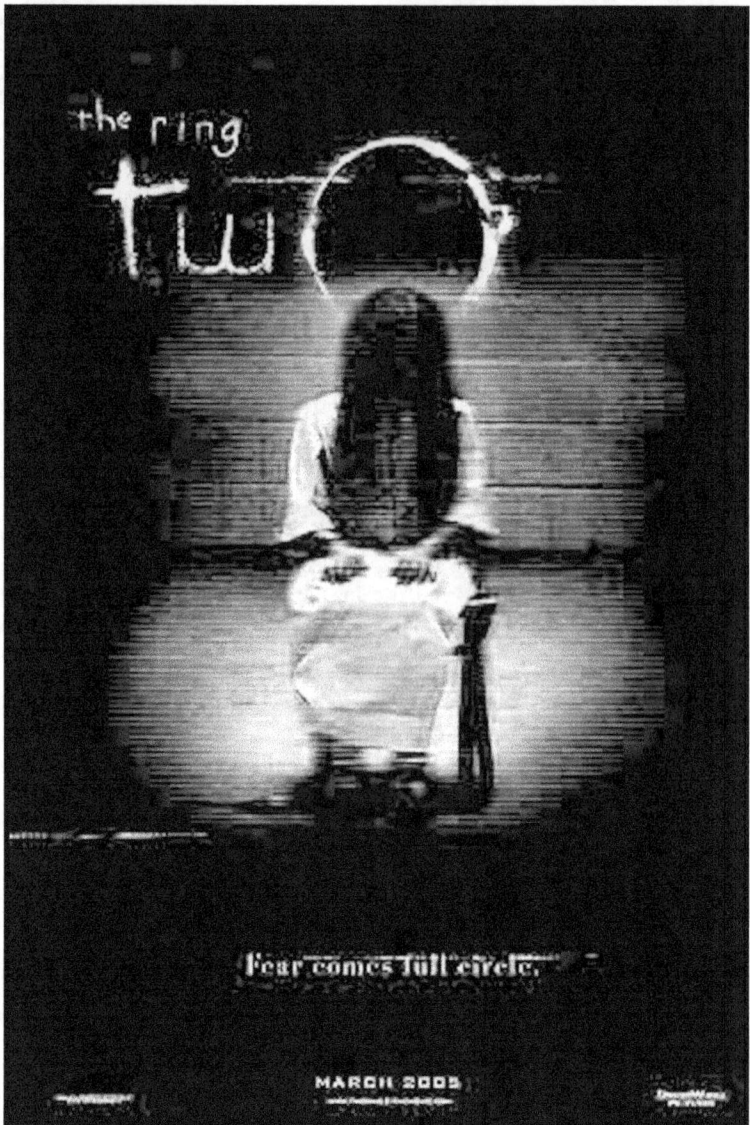

The film's publicity cheats by playing up the participation of Sissy Spacek, who portrays a demented mother confined to an institution who rants and raves all so seriously. Her performance amounts to a quick cameo that does not warrant such attention and billing.

*The Ring Two* still has snatches of the original videotape and Samara creeping about both in and out of her tomb-like television set. However, the film's best sequence seems almost out of context, but it works beautifully. In a startling montage of horror, Kelly and Aidan are driving in their vehicle in a wooded area when a deer suddenly runs in front of the car and is hit. Soon innocent-looking deer gather by the roadside, at first one, then several, and pretty soon many deer totally surround the vehicle. Aidan quietly commands they drive away, but mother Kelly is transfixed by this weird display of nature. But shockingly two deer butt the doors of the car from both sides, ramming their heads hard into the car's frame. Glass shatters and the doors buckle, and the surround sound makes the head butts sound like atomic explosions. After this initial attack, broken glass everywhere, Kelly does rev up her car and speeds away, killing all deer who stand in her path. Such an odd and quirky sequence becomes the

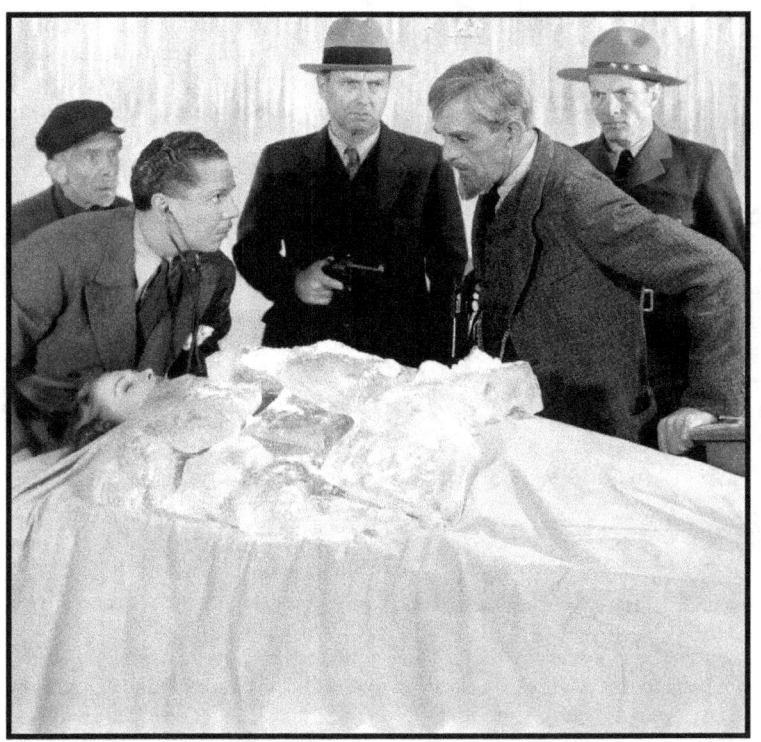

most memorable sequence of horror. It rivals the horse sequence from the first American *The Ring*.

Besides a pristine unrated print with fabulous sound, *The Ring Two* features a short film, *Rings,* that connects *The Ring* with *The Ring Two* (although the short is not directed by Hideo Nakata, it stars the actors from the beginning sequence of *The Ring Two*) and features deleted scenes and two documentaries, one of which is a fascinating analysis of the visual symbols used in the film. *The Ring Two,* while a solid sequel, once again demonstrates how directors can use atmospheric chills to generate goose bumps that get under the skin and continually creep you out.

**The Man With Nine Lives**
Movie: 3.0; Disc: 3.5
[Columbia/TriStar]

Last year *The Devil Commands* came to DVD, first of the anticipated Columbia Mad Doctor series of the late 1930s/early 1940s to be released to the home video market. *The Devil Commands* was the best of the batch of four movies, but many fans always considered *The Man With Nine Lives* to be the pride of the litter. While *The Man With Nine Lives* is a riveting B production, it pales in comparison to *The Devil Commands*.

In *The Man With Nine Lives* Boris Karloff portrays Dr. Kravaal, a researcher in freeze therapy seeking a cure for cancer, a doctor discovered frozen in ice 10 years after his disappearance. The film opens in an operating theater where Dr. Mason (Roger Pryor) demonstrates surgery based upon the work of Dr. Kravaal. Then the film switches locations and moves to the Canadian border cabin in Silverlake where Kravaal disappeared. The rest of the film remains not only at the cabin, but for the most part in the basement of that cabin that contains two ice chambers. Thus, the action is very claustrophobic with the setting so limited. Karloff's Kravaal is sympathetic but one note. He is working to save the life of a patient that he froze, and the man's nephew, along with the law, accuse the scientist of murder and order his arrest. Using poison gas Kravaal tries to overcome his mob-like jury and executioners, but all are trapped inside an ice cavern and frozen to death. Ironically, the patient survives but dies left unattended in the outer room. Ten years pass and Dr. Mason and his romantic interest, also his nurse (Jo Ann Sayers), thaw out the doctor and his accusers. It seems the poison concoction allowed for humans to be frozen and yet continue to live after being thawed, but the irate nephew destroys the formula that Kravaal wrote down by throwing the paper into the fire. Kravaal immediately shoots and kills the idiot. However, hoping to replicate the formula, Kravaal uses the human guinea pigs as test cases, but they all die. Last but not least, Mason and his nurse become the final guinea pigs to be tested.

Karloff's character of Kravaal changes from sympathetic experimenter to obsessed and half-crazed scientist who is willing to sacrifice the lives of humans for the cause of science. Karloff's character changes in *The Devil Commands* were more pronounced and interesting. He even altered his hair-do to illustrate the extent of his change. *The Devil Commands*, occurring mostly in his haunted country estate, did not feel so confining as the limited sets of *The Man With Nine Lives*. The character interaction in *The Man With Nine Lives* is not well defined, with most of the characters becoming stereotypes of one kind or another. We have the good-hearted nurse, the good doctor, the obsessed/insane doctor, the sheriff, the irate nephew, all of whom are in conflict. Nowhere is there to be found the brain-damaged buffoon of *The Devil Commands*, the evil spiritualist played by Anne Revere or any of the interesting off-kiltered characters from that production. When it comes to moody cinematography, *The Devil Commands* features a haunted mansion with shadowy entrances and exits and a crazy laboratory filled with corpses wearing metallic headgear. It's simply a more outrageous production. *The Man With Nine Lives* features mountain cabins and ice chambers and lacks the iconic horror aspects to make it a production that stands out.

Bottom line, *The Man With Nine Lives* is a solid B programmer with an interesting Boris Karloff performance

and novel plot involving cryogenics a generation before reports surfaced that Walt Disney was frozen at the time of his death. Both it and *The Devil Commands* are superior to the other two productions in the Mad Doctor series, but *The Devil Commands* still remains the superior entry. For all fans of classic horror, *The Man With Nine Lives* is a blessing nonetheless, presented here with a nice transfer with deep blacks and effective contrast.

**The Bela Lugosi Collection**
Movie: *Murders in the Rue Morgue* (2.5); *The Black Cat* (3.5); *The Raven* (3.0); *Invisible Ray* (3.5); *Black Friday* (2.5); Disc: 3.5
[Universal]

After the success of The Legacy horror film series (collecting all the Frankenstein movies, Dracula movies, Invisible Man Movies, Gill Man movies, etc.), it was about time for non-series 1930s horror classics to come to DVD. When *The Black Cat* and *The Raven* were released to laser disc a decade ago, they were not remastered and the films were slightly sped up so each would fit on a 60-minute laserdisc side.

First the good news. All five movies have been restored/remastered and look the best they ever looked on home video, and the actual running times of the formerly sped up classics have been restored. Once again the package is one of extreme delight for the DVD collector, featuring a close-up of Bela Lugosi with gatefold packaging for the single disc (which houses all five movies over both sides). Now the bad news. Because all five movies are pressed on a single disc (not a problem on the earlier Legacy series which featured multiple-disc presentations) which increases the compression used to master the movies, collectors have reported that many DVD players (not just one or two) cannot successfully play the movies, that the picture will pixilate and freeze at specific points while watching specific titles. *The Raven* seems to be a major offender. Also, for fans of Boris Karloff, Boris Karloff is the star in four of these movies (*Murders in the Rue Morgue* is the only film in which only Bela Lugosi appears), so why call the collection *The Bela Lugosi Collection*? And finally the only extras are theatrical trailers for three of the five movies. In other words, Universal, unlike Warner Bros., seems to care very little about these classic movies that helped establish their studio. Instead of releasing five movies on two discs that would have negated the compression problems, Universal decided to create the first box set on a single platter. How rude!

First, let us examine *The Raven*, the often-underrated 1935 movie directed by Lew Landers. Of all the films in the collection starring Karloff and Lugosi, *The Raven* is the only one that features Lugosi in a role that overshadows Karloff's performance. And Lugosi's portrayal of Dr. Vollin is in many ways his best performance in a non-character role (i.e., Ygor). Never has Lugosi looked more handsome or distinguished, and his line delivery is much more natural than it was in *Dracula*. His demented personality housing both the distinguished surgeon and the depraved psychopath has never been better displayed. *The Raven* offers a tour de force performance by Bela Lugosi. And Lugosi's progression into lunacy is amaz-

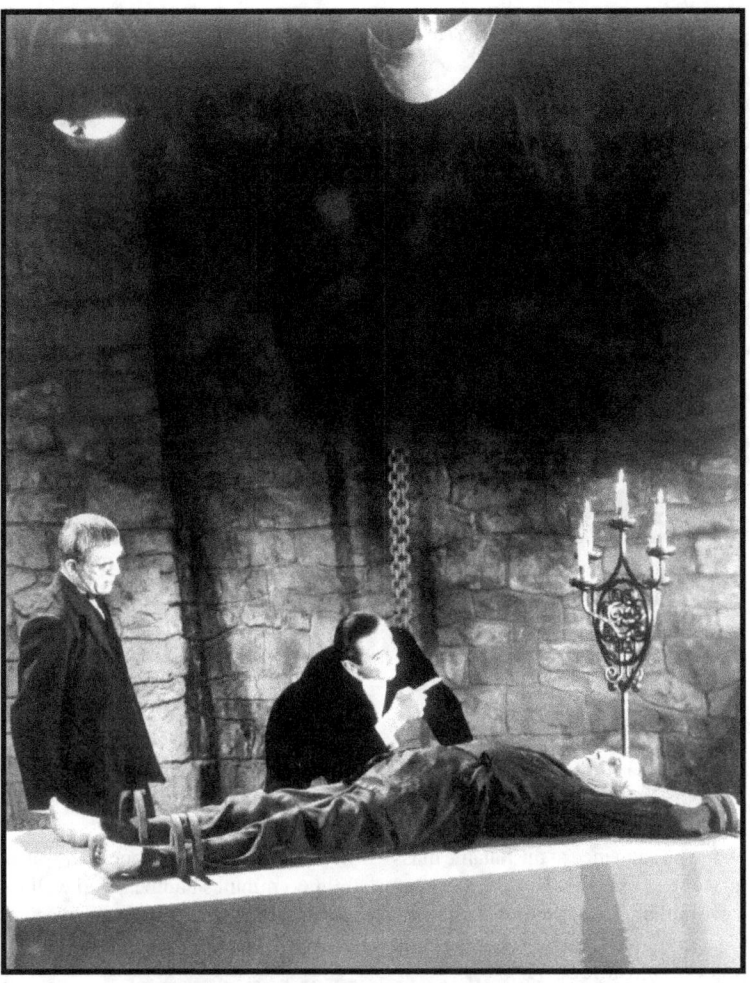

ing. We first meet him when Judge Thatcher (Samuel S. Hines) implores the now retired surgeon to operate on his daughter Jean (Irene Ware) to save her life. The doctor is firm in his refusal until Thatcher admits the other surgeons stated that Vollin would be the best man for the job, and then his overblown ego kicks in and he agrees to operate. Soon we see the grateful and fully recovered Jean repeatedly thank Vollin by dedicating her new dance recital (she is a professional dancer) to Edgar Allan Poe, Vollin's idol. But when Jean mentions her fiancé, the sexually obsessed surgeon shows his true colors and makes it known he expects the young girl to thank him in the marriage bed. Vollin will settle for no less.

Soon Vollin invites the Judge, Jean and her fiancé (Lester Matthews) to his home for a dinner party, with a few other guests in attendance. The house, ornate and opulent in its excess, is revealed to have secret passageways, rooms that move up and down from level to level, torture chambers in the cellar, etc. Before long the Judge is shackled to a slab with a pendulum blade swinging closer and closer to his heart while Jean is kidnapped. In a splendid over-the-top performance, Vollin states torturing others is the only cure for the mental torture he faces in losing the love of his life to another man. In wonderful sequences, Lugosi flails his arms and shakes them about, cackles like a madman, throws his hands over his eyes and falls forward, landing fast and hard on his knees. His is a physical and eccentric performance that simply works in his outrageousness and clearly exemplifies why Bela Lugosi is such a cherished horror film personality.

Karloff as Bateman, a rough and tumble gangster in need of a new face fast, is best in his initial sequences when he pleads for Vollin to help him, even at the point of a gun. And after the operation is finished, the safely protected Vollin, looking at and speaking to Bateman through a grille in the ceiling, demands that Bateman become his servant in order for him to fix his paralyzed face. Unfortunately, for the rest of the movie, Karloff does little more than obey the beck and call of Vollin. *The Raven* is truly Bela Lugosi's movie, and when examined

**Midnight Marquee 75**

in this excellently remastered print, the movie looks better than it ever has.

Perhaps Edgar Ulmer's eccentric classic *The Black Cat* is the best film in the collection, and with its themes of Satanism, war atrocities, embalming one's wife and putting her body on display in the cellar and skinning one's enemy alive, *The Black Cat* proves that Universal horror can be cutting edge and absolutely quirky. But for me *The Black Cat*'s most important aspect is that it teamed Karloff (as he was billed) and Bela Lugosi together for the first time and established the concept of icon horror movie stars. Karloff and Lugosi have never been better together, and what is even more rare, their character roles are equally important and share a balanced screen time.

*The Black Cat* truly deserves a director's cut, for what survives has been truncated by Universal and the film looks it. In little more than an hour of screen time, director Ulmer establishes the hatred between Poelzig (Karloff) and Werdegast (Lugosi) based upon the love of the same woman, Lugosi's wife, whose beautifully preserved corpse hangs suspended in a glass case, along with the bodies of other beautiful women. Unknown to Werdegast, the evil war criminal Poelzig married Werdegast's daughter Karen, but the sinister Poelzig tells Werdegast both mother and daughter are dead. Poelzig is responsible for Werdegast spending 15 years in a prisoner-of-war camp, and the more than slightly weirded-out Werdegast (casting Lugosi as almost the hero) has returned for revenge. Unfortunately, mystery writer Peter Alison (David Manners in one of his best roles) and wife Joan (Jacqueline Welles), slightly injured in a bus accident, are the pawns in this chess game of revenge (played both literally and figuratively), the chessboard metaphor becoming Poelzig's modernistic fortress home. Poelzig, leader of a Satanic cult, intends to sacrifice the unsuspecting Joan on his sacrificial altar, and her body will most likely be on display in the glass case in the cellar before long. Werdegast, besides exacting revenge on the demon in human form who ruined his life, also intends to save the lives of the innocent Alisons.

Featuring so many classic sequences, *The Black Cat* is classic Karloff and Lugosi all the way. For instance, Karloff shines in his initial sequence where he rises, stiffly and quickly erect, from a prone position in bed. The sequence at the Satanic mass is wonderful, with Karloff wearing his ritualistic robe, tall and thin, his v-shaped widow's peak pronounced and only adding an image of evil to his character. Lugosi shines when he first confronts Werdegast and drones on about the 15 lost years of his life. And when Karloff shows him his perfectly preserved wife in glass, Lugosi breaks down emotionally in a tenderly real reaction sequence. After Lugosi is shot in the film's climax, he calls his attackers fools and yet still does whatever he can to save their lives. A twisted majesty exists to Lugosi's performance, the sense of a decent man bent by the evil course of events in his life who still shows both extremes of compassion and insanity in equal measures throughout the production. And Karloff's Poelzig has never been more cruel, eventually murdering his own wife, Werdegast's daughter, rather than allowing father and daughter to unite and share one moment of peace.

*The Black Cat* speeds by at a tight 66 minutes and bears up well to repeated viewings, showcasing that

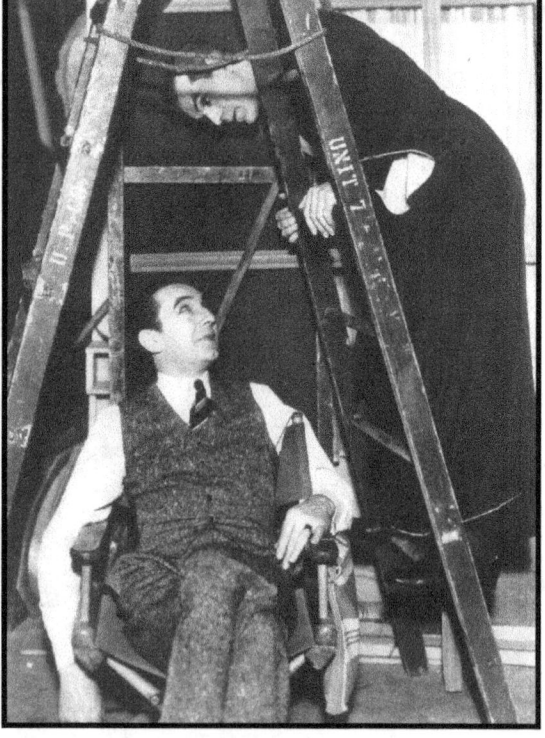

Universal horror can include much, much more than classic monsters and that the most flesh-and-blood human monsters can sometimes be the most frightening. Boris Karloff and Bela Lugosi demonstrate the extent of their acting talents by creating characters and performances that are so off kilter that they reasonate for generations to come.

Far less successful a movie, but looking beautiful here restored, is Robert Florey's "prize" for losing *Frankenstein* to James Whale, *Murders in the Rue Morgue*. This 1932 production is the only movie that does not feature Boris Karloff in the collection, and thus the reason why the box set can be called *The Bela Lugosi Collection*. Lugosi's performance as Dr. Mirakle, ever the cheap carnival charlatan, is magnificent and textured. However, the supporting cast and script disappoints. Lugosi's scientist wishes to prove that apes share a familiarity of background with humans and that injecting a beautiful young woman with the blood of Erik the ape may prove such a connection. Unfortunately, all the human victims die because their blood is not "pure." Of course when Mirakle's fog-shrouded carriage comes upon a common woman of the streets (Arlene Francis), a woman he kidnaps, well, of course her blood is not pure, and after she dies while strapped to a wooden sacrificial cross, her body is dumped to the river below by servant Noble Johnson, in white face, who plays servant Janos the Black One. The image of Lugosi in his mad lab, a sexy whore writhing in fear tied to his cross in classic bondage style, with a gorilla close by, contains dramatic iconic elements making this sequence a classic one in horror film history. And the sequence is truly spectacular. But when we cut back and forth to bland sequences featuring the truly awful Sidney Fox as heroine Camille, overdone hero Leon Waycoff (soon to be Ames) and horrible comic relief Bert Roach as Paul, the film becomes bogged down in banality.

The film's climax is wonderful, featuring the ape carrying Sidney Fox under its arm across the rooftops of Paris with lover Dupin in close pursuit. The film's main distraction is the inter-cutting of the actor-in-a-suit with close-up shots of actual ape heads. Somewhere the juxtaposing of Hollywood ape and actual animal just does not jive and is rather disconcerting. The film's rooftop chase is thrilling, and when the ape is shot and rolls off the side of the roof into the river, all seems well in this Universal fairy-tale land. The film's basic plot is ridiculous and the acting second-rate. Florey's direction is sometimes too gimmicky, depending upon razzle-dazzle shots of people in the park playing on swings with the camera panning up and down. Generally, as has been true for most of his long career, when Lugosi is onscreen the film shines, but when Lugosi disap-

pears the shortcomings of the film and all its weaknesses show through. However, for 1932 the print is pristine and looks simply fabulous.

Perhaps the unsung gem of the set is the always-underrated *The Invisible Ray*, which happens to be one of my favorite Universal horror movies (although its genesis is more by way of science fiction) and features equal performances (both stellar) by Boris Karloff and Bela Lugosi. For one thing, *The Invisible Ray* has a sense of scope. We start at Janos Rukh's home observatory, then move to the African jungle and finally end up in the city of Paris with Rukh running amok. The character of Rukh is classic Karloff, at first illustrating the scientist to be the dedicated man of science, but soon his nobility fades as he is revealed to be an anti-social recluse who feels paranoid about his scientific discovery, quickly reverting, via the help of Radium X poisoning, into an avenging madman who methodically kills those people he holds responsible for stealing his discovery. Via John Fulton's inspired glowing special effects, Karloff radiates in the darkness and his simple touch spells instant death, unless he takes the antidote given him by his doubting Thomas rival Dr. Benet (Bela Lugosi). Karloff is sympathetic and deranged, while Lugosi, looking majestic in slicked-back hair and goatee, underplays his performance but still generates conflicting flashes of both ruthless detachment and compassion. The teaming of these horror icons is both inspired and totally satisfying, with neither actor upstaging the other and both performances becoming important ones.

The best sequences in the movie involve the teaming of Karloff and Violet Kemble Cooper as Mother Rukh, the stern white-haired woman who tells her son he is not good dealing with people and should work alone in his laboratory. She is absolutely correct, but her lack of motherly sympathy and her hard-nosed life lessons make her a truly fascinating character. At the movie's end when Janos confronts her pleading for comfort and advice, she flings her cane

and smashes the bottle of antidote, spelling her son's destruction when he turns momentarily into a human fireball and burns away. Even among veterans, Cooper contributes a performance equal to Karloff and Lugosi (albeit of much shorter duration).

For years people have criticized the direction of Lambert Hillyer, who is best known for directing B productions and serials. For me the charm of *The Invisible Ray* is its outrageous sense of sci-fi adventure theatrics. The movie contains complex characters with delicate problems. For instance, Rukh's wife Diana (Frances Drake) is much younger than he and admits she only married Rukh because her father, Rukh's now dead assistant, admired the scientist and wanted her to marry him (Freud would do wonders with these relationships). But Hillyer keeps the action pumping and the plot marching onward. Besides the jungle footage discovering and harnessing Radium X, we also have the sidebar story of Rukh's wife falling for the young hunk in the pith helmet (Ronald Drake), thus explaining Rukh's impending insanity: He loses both his scientific formula and wife in one hot and muggy expedition (where all the actors are constantly sweating). But once Rukh disappears and is presumed dead, the real fun begins as the demented avenging angel methodically kills each member of the expedition, one at a time. For once a film's pacing and performances go hand in hand to produce an outstanding Universal horror epic that is long overdue to be recognized as the wonderful chiller it most certainly is. And as stated, Karloff and Lugosi have never been better balanced. Also, it is indeed refreshing to see Boris Karloff create a broad, over-the-top performance that rivals or betters Lugosi's similar broad performances.

Last, and certainly least, is *Black Friday*, released in 1940 and the most modern production released in this collection. While *Black Friday* is rare enough and deserves such a restored DVD release as it's given here, I would have much preferred an even rarer title such as *Night Monster* to be included. And once again *Night Monster* stars a solo Bela Lugosi in one of his best B programmers from the 1940s. But *Black Friday* offers Karloff and Lugosi in performances that were changed a short while before production began. So Stanley Ridges, as the benevolent college professor who inherits the brain of a criminal mastermind, steals the show. Bela Lugosi, puffy-faced and wearing black, brings a less than original take to the 1940s gangster arena with his portrayal of Eric Marnay. And the

stereotypical sympathetic Dr. Sovac presents Boris Karloff with another by-the-numbers performance that shines by nature of the actor's overwhelming talent. The film works best in its opening minutes when we see Sovac, framed by prison bars and sitting in the shadows, awaiting his execution for murder. Handing his notebook to a young reporter as he passes by on the long walk to oblivion, he calmly tells the reporter that his newspaper gave the most fair coverage of the trial, and, in a handwritten note, he wishes his research will serve the needs of mankind. The zippy quick-cuts punctuated with crescendoing musical cues give *Black Friday* a visual style that is all but forgotten once the movie becomes a standard story told in flashbacks.

*Black Friday* would have been better if Karloff or Lugosi portrayed the professor role enacted by Ridges, but the truth is that Ridges probably played the role better than either icon and this fact probably angers most critics who view the film as somewhat of an aborted effort. As released, Lugosi is little more than supporting player and Karloff is doing a performance he could phone in in his sleep. And Ridges creates a Jekyll and Hyde bravura performance, while the two horror icons are reduced to bland support. It is impossible to watch *Black Friday* and not think about what other role Karloff and Lugosi should be playing. It's not that *Black Friday* is bad; it is simply generic. Yes, it is probably better than *The Mad Ghoul* because of its star power and extra budget, but it's barely better. After *The Raven*, *The Black Cat* and *The Invisible Ray,* fans expected and deserved better.

Even when considering the problems resulting with mastering these titles with too much compression, *The Bela Lugosi Collection* is one of the year's marvels, even if mistitled and done on the cheap without extras. Never have these Universal classics looked or sounded this good, and hopefully similar releases from Universal will be forthcoming in the upcoming year.

**Land of the Dead**
Movie: 3.0; Disc: 3.5
[Universal]

Director George Romero has been floundering for two decades since the release of *Day of the Dead*, the third installment in his classic zombie trilogy. Most Romero fans felt rather cool toward *Day of the Dead*, thinking it lacked the audacity and balls-out horror of *Dawn of the Dead*. For me, *Dawn of the Dead*, while a riveting and well-produced horror epic, was, let's be honest, over-indulgent and way too long. The film's unnatural shifts in tone, from the outrageous splatter, to the nightmarishly frightening, to the almost silly encounter with Tom Savini's motorcycle gang, left a rather unsettled feeling. *Day of the Dead* was the smarter movie, it was more tightly scripted and executed. It lacked some of the audacity of *Dawn of the Dead*, but the plot to me was even more intriguing and tried to offer more blatant social criticism. Unfortunately the box-office for *Day of the Day* was not stellar, and the zombie trilogy ended with just that... a trilogy.

While everyone was anticipating a *Twilight of the Dead*, instead Universal financed Romero's first zombie movie since 1983, a film to be called *Land of the Dead*. Fortunately and unfortunately, Romero's movie was bankrolled based upon a mini-zombie resurgence fueled mainly by the big-budget remake of *Dawn of the Dead*, the intriguing *28 Days Later* and the sophisticated and intelligent *Shaun of the Dead*, which raised zombie social consciousness to a new level. What better time for the old veteran to return to the flesh-eating arena by producing his fourth zombie entry. The disappointment noted above stems from the simple fact that *Land of the Dead*, while a solid production, is the least of Romero's zombie movies and pales in comparison to the three films mentioned above.

To its betterment, *Land of the Dead* features the largest budget Romero ever obtained for a horror movie. Just like when director/writer John Waters entered the mainstream, gone is Romero's house production company, with Tom Savini relegated to a cameo Machete Zombie appearance. Instead his new crew comprises current special effects companies headed by veterans such as Greg Nicotero. Romero, by nature of his calling card, is expected to feature protracted sequences of human victims being disemboweled by zombie

predators, and while the effects never disappoint, they do create the sense of deja-vu/been-here-done-that sameness. The best zombie effect is one living dead warrior, his head hanging over the back of his body, held to his spine by literally a fleshy thread. In one of the best shock sequences, the head snaps back onto the neck with zombie teeth gnashing away, soon claiming human flesh and blood.

For once Romero seems to have assembled a truly professional cast of actors, led by marquee exploitation star Asia Argento (daughter of Dario, the major producer for Romero's *Dawn of the Dead*) who looks slightly past her prime in this production (heavy lines under her eyes and a puffiness to her face). However, her physical butt-kicking performance jump-starts the production. On the male side we have hero Simon Baker (as Riley) and sidekick oddity Charlie (a wonderful Robert Joy), whose fire-scarred half-a-face leaves him with one dead eye that makes him the perfect marksman. Simply, the rapport between Riley and Charlie is always interesting, demonstrating male camaraderie at its warmest and most loyal. And even Dennis Hopper comes along for the ride as the rich and (of course) corrupted Kaufman. Hopper's performance is nothing new for the versatile actor, but his professional sense of rhythm and line delivery is just interesting to observe. And of course Romero gives Hopper an explosive death sequence (too bad he is not eaten alive by the living dead).

Once again the plot is not Shakespeare; however, Romero is still obsessed with the haves and have-nots, belittling the military guardians who save the asses of the rich, only to be denied the right to purchase an apartment in their luxury high rise (John Leguizamo's performance is based upon attempting to buy himself the good life, and when that life he earned is denied, for the rest of the movie Leguizamo is focused on revenge). In this film the zombies are beginning to learn how to survive and how to become human again. Black actor Eugene Clark as Big Daddy illustrates this newfound intelligence. *Land of the Dead*'s money sequence is where Big Daddy leads his zombie warriors to the high rise city by marching his troops underwater (first only their heads and shoulders pop out of the water, then their entire bodies emerge) with haunting intensity. It's a marvelous sequence.

Unfortunately, I cannot say that *Land of the Dead* tops *Shaun of the Dead* or the new *Dawn of the Dead*, but it definitely is a movie worth viewing. It will most likely be considered the lesser of Romero's zombie series, but after a 20-year hibernation, it is just dandy to see the grizzled indie warrior come back with a solid horror movie that still has a political statement to make. A character states near the movie's end, zombies, like the majority of humans, are simply trying to find their place in the world. Of

course supplemental features include an audio commentary, several documentaries, zombie casting calls and an examination of the storyboards. All in all, a worthy package for a worthy movie created by a writer/director who can now be called a veteran of horror cinema.

### The Hammer Horror Franchise Collection

Movies: *Brides of Dracula* (3.5); *Curse of the Werewolf* (3.0); *Phantom of the Opera* (2.5); *Paranoiac* (3.0); *Kiss of the Vampire* (3.0); *Nightmare* (2.5); *Night Creatures* (2.5); *Evil of Frankenstein* (3.0); Disc: 3.0
[Universal]

After *Curse of Frankenstein* hit American shores (released by Warner Bros.), Universal and Columbia became the primary distributors of Hammer horror during the decade following. Amazingly, all the Universal Hammer releases, with one glaring exception, have been released to one discount-priced two-disc DVD collection.

The good thing is that because of the two-disc set holding eight features, the street price is about $25. However, because Universal used both sides of both discs and increased the amount of compression to squeeze so many movies per side, many DVD players have experienced problems playing these discs with pixilation and freeze-ups occurring. However, many people returned the initial purchased set and reported second copies obtained played flawlessly, or nearly so. Once again Universal needs to hear that people are willing to pay higher prices to obtain these movies, as long as they play flawlessly on DVD players both old and new.

Unfortunately, the Hammer classic for all time *Horror of Dracula* was sold to Warner Bros. in the mid-1960s so it could be re-released on a double-bill with *Curse of Frankenstein*. Last year Warners released *Horror of Dracula* to DVD by omitting the Universal globe at the beginning and releasing the movie in the wrong aspect ratio, thus cutting off the tops of objects and heads. *Horror of Dracula* would have looked gorgeous if it were included with the rest of the set here, mastered in its original (and correct) aspect ratio. But this was not to be. And so such a Universal Hammer box set is seriously flawed already.

Instead, this fabulous Universal collection, while it excludes extras such as documentaries and audio commentaries, includes pristine mastering of most of the movies and all are released at their proper aspect ratios, making them the ultimate Hammer collection. And all eight features cost about $3.00 each!

First, the set begins with the masterpiece *Brides of Dracula*, a film worthy of being in my top-10 horror classics of all time, but a film nevertheless inferior to the greatest Hammer production of all time, *Horror of Dracula*. Revisionist theory now holds *Brides of Dracula* being superior, and while it is a superior movie in itself, it is too derivative of *Horror of Dracula* to be called the better film. David Peel is one of the finest movie vampires, with his gray cape, flaming red hair (not adequately captured on this DVD release; while the color reproduction is excellent, the hues are not as dramatic as the original Tech prints) and deliberate line readings, but he is just not Christopher Lee. Let me support my claim. David Peel's performance includes two extreme variations in his character of Baron Meinster. First he is the brooding, romantic Byronic hero (the shackled man who stands on his castle ledge, apparently ready to jump; the handsome young man who comes to visit Marianne at her teaching academy). Second, he is the bestial vampire (with his well-kempt hair becoming more frizzy, his eyes bulging, his evil sneer radiating and a mouthful of fangs flashing). However, when he confronts Gina (Andree Melly) to vampirize her, he appears in the animalistic stage with little attempt made to romance the almost willing victim. After courting and romancing Marianne (Yvonne Monlaur), he storms into her room and takes her by force. Here is Peel's major flaw… he can play both extremes effectively but lacks the subtlety to effortlessly meld one into the other. Christopher Lee cold be the animalistic vampire (during the brutal library entrance) and the dashing romantic (his early sequences with Harker), but when he seduces both Mina and Lucy, we see layers of both extremes in his performance. Peel's performance lacks this depth.

*Brides of Dracula* has perhaps the faster-paced and more effective rhythm throughout, but *Horror of Dracula* contains more outstanding sequences. In *Brides of Dracula* we have Van Helsing (Peter Cushing's performance in both films is perhaps the most outstanding in his career and he is equally impressive in both) returning to the chateau to confront the Baron in a shorter rehash of the climax to *Horror of Dracula*. This is followed by the wonderful sequence with Martita Hunt where she reveals his incestuous relationship to her own son the Baron. And we have the superb windmill sequence with the two vampires protected by their nurse Greta (Freda Jackson in a wondrous over-the-top performance) before the Baron appears. These are *Brides of Dracula*'s money sequences (along with perhaps the eerie resurrection sequence of Marie Devereux coaxed by the vampiric mid-wife Greta). *Horror of Dracula* features the nightmarish sequence where Harker goes alone into Dracula's crypt and kills Dracula's mate Valerie Gaunt, failing to kill the Count before sunset. Then we have the landmark sequence in the library where Harker is infected. Finally we have the outstanding climax where Van Helsing chases Count Dracula throughout his castle and ultimately destroys him in the blinding sunlight. And did I almost forget the subtlety and dread in the sequence where vampiric Lucy attempts to seduce her young sister Tania but is dramatically foiled by the sudden intervention of Van Helsing? *Horror of Dracula* has endless sequences that are simply superior to those outstanding sequences in *Brides of Dracula*. And so many of the best scenes from *Brides of Dracula* are obviously mod-

eled after the similar sequences from the originator. Simply compare the pulse-pounding climax from *Horror of Dracula* to the disappointing one from *Brides of Dracula*… a short fight with the Baron, holy water acid in the face and finally the shadow of the windmill in the shadow of a cross. Second rate all the way when compared to its predecessor.

But while this revisionist theory of the superiority of *Brides of Dracula* has obviously colored this review, I must state that both films are in my top 10 and both reflect the absolute best work created by director Terence Fisher whose world of vampires is unholy, other-human and the finest realization of the world of the undead yet captured on film. While other vampire films go for the gusto, the dramatic, the special effects and the over-acted, Terence Fisher's vampires are subtle, multi-layered, sensual and pathetic (and horrifying), all at the same time. The use of glarish Technicolor photography to embellish this world of fairy-tale depravity only helps to capture this cinematic world of the undead to perfection. And *Brides of Dracula*, with its photography, Technicolor, direction and performances becomes a classic for all time.

The other vampire film in this collection is 1963's *Kiss of the Vampire*, directed (unfortunately) by Don Sharp, a film inferior to *Brides of Dracula* (but the gap in quality is greater between *Brides* and *Kiss* than was the gap between *Horrror* and *Brides*) mostly because Don Sharp's vision of vampirism is at times too imitative of Terence Fisher's and at other times too flat and literal without all the wonderful visual layers of Fish-

er's vampiric world. Let me state this, with the pristine print and wonderfully restored Eastmancolor (lacking the starkness of Technicolor), *Kiss of the Vampire* is a solidly entertaining Hammer vampire movie filled with a few marvelous performances (especially Edward de Sousa as Gerald, one of the finest Hammer heroes, with a performance that requires him to play drunk, romantic bliss, fear of insanity and the horror of confronting vampirism). While *Kiss of the Vampire* appears fifth on the set, it is the first of the films to feature a musical score by James Bernard, and his piano sonata is one of his finest contributions to horror cinema, as the overall score also excels. Perhaps the set direction by Bernard Robinson (featuring both the interior of the castle and the hotel interior) is among his finest work. And the script, no longer created by Jimmy Sangster but now by John Elder (Anthony Hinds), is mysterious and haunting. But where is the wonderful pacing of a Terence Fisher film (too much time is spent with the newlyweds' motor car breaking down and the couple entering and meeting the proprietors of the hotel)? Where are the outstanding horror sequences? Where is the sense of the vampires as undead (the brother and sister who travel by coach and hide beneath parasols, only to rush back to their protective carriage, hurriedly pulling down the purple shades, comes closest to capturing this sense of the undead)? Noel Willman as Dr. Ravna is very subtle and quite effective as the leader of the vampire cult (although one's eyes constantly go to his hair extensions that embellish his widow's peak), but he is definitely a vampire cast in the actors-who-resemble-Christopher-Lee mold. And while Willman's underplaying works very nicely, he is definitely *not* Christopher Lee.

Most disappointing is the lack of a Van Helsing or powerful vampire hunter in the mold that Peter Cushing made a Hammer staple. Instead Clifford Evans (recently seen as the father from *Curse of the Werewolf*) portrays Professor Zimmer, a drunken shell of a burned-out man who lives in solitude, mysteriously appearing at the most opportune times to sniff out the undead. If we had a back-story or some evidence of a characterization to make the audience care about this broken man, his performance might have resonated and been more profound. Now he is the gruff man who appears out of nowhere to provide the necessary help. Even his pivotal sequence confronting the evil vampire Tania (Isobel Black), who is attempting a vampiric resurrection sequence similar to the one performed by Freda Jackson in *Brides of Dracula,* is truncated and cheaply shot, substituting mountains of fog for a carefully rendered set. When Zimmer confronts the sensual vampire girl, he is bitten on the hand and forced to stick his hand in fire, repeating the similar branding sequence from *Brides of Dracula*, but to far less effect.

*Kiss of the Vampire* shines most brightly in sequences such as its masquerade party at Ravna's castle, where all the party guests are members of Ravna's cult and their mission is to get Gerald's wife Marianne (even the name comes from *Brides of Dracula*) alone with Ravna, so he can seduce and initiate her into the cult of the undead. Poor Gerald is given too much to drink and is finally drugged to keep him out of the way, and when he awakens he is accused of being drunk and unruly and no one knows anything about his wife having ever attended the party. The production design of Ravna's sleeping quarters, housing his coffin, is spectacular, and Willman's subtle seduction of Marianne (Jennifer Daniel), having her lie down on a mat before he strokes and bites her, is very effective (although Don Sharp enjoys focusing on vampire's mouths and slightly shifting the lens to out-of-focus once or twice too often). Later the audience sees she is totally nude (although we see her photographed from the back, from the waist up, so only the illusion of nudity is created) as Ravna dresses her in her ceremonial white robe before presenting her as a new disciple to the other cult members. The concept of the vampire cult is fresh and original, but more is needed by again creating a back-story of the cult, its origins, its purpose and how Ravna became its leader. Once again Elder and Sharp rely too much on costume and set design when we need a plot to connect the dots. But most importantly, the horror mood is there.

My favorite sequence is the one at Ravna's castle where Gerald gets to see his wife, now mesmerized and vampirized, and Ravna confidently orders Marianne to prove she no longer loves her husband (she demonstrates this by spitting in his face). Then, the nympho vampire Tania savagely rips the shirt off Gerald's back, claws his exposed chest with her fingernails and playfully teases the man, all in front of his wife, before Tania pounces downward to pierce his neck, but he pushes her away at the last moment and paints a cross on his chest with his own blood, grabs Marianne, and escapes with the help of Zimmer. It's a marvelous sequence filled with perversity, horror and punctuated with tension. However *Brides of Dracula* contained three or four such sequences, while *Kiss of the Vampire* contains a precious few.

*Kiss of the Vampire*'s audacity is put to the test during its climactic vampire ritual, where Zimmer draws a magic circle in chalk and casts a spell (during the cycle of the full moon when Saturn is in the proper position, no less) forcing evil to turn against itself. In this spell vampire bats are evoked from Hell to attack the cult and drain the vampires of their life's blood. Unfortunately the big-budgeted Hitchcock classic *The Birds* was made the same year and showed what could be done via special effects involving bird attacks. The Hammer bat attacks were of course cheaply concocted and far less effective, and *Kiss of the Vampire* has been criticized for its climax ever since. To be quite honest, on this DVD release, the bat

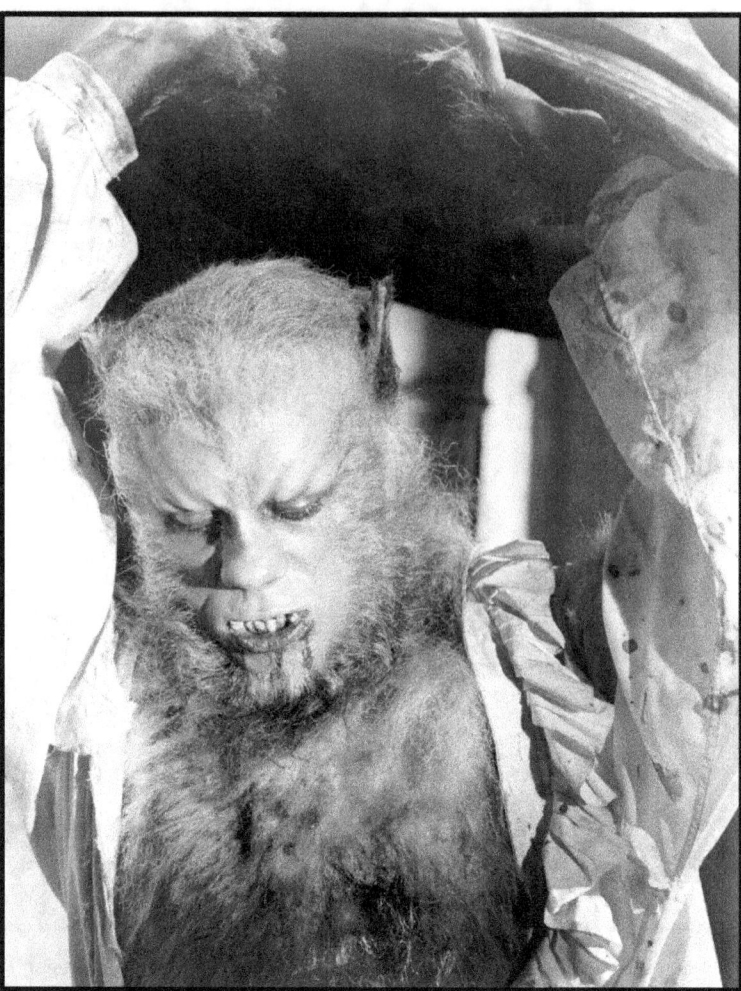

attack works reasonably well, and with inter-cuts of flailing bare legs, plunging necklines and snatches of woman's underwear appearing here and there, for any adolescent male, the special effects are more than highly successful.

In the hands of Terence Fisher, the other-worldly mood of the world of vampires would have been more consistently powerful, but Don Sharp's direction is quite adequate, yet seldom inspired. Noel Willman, Edward de Sousa and Isobel Black perform with enthusiasm, yet other performances are hampered, not necessarily by lack of thespic talent, but more often by the sketchy script. More often Elder's script contains lack of motivation and back-story and the resulting performances appear half-baked. For instance, the subplot with the kindly innkeepers and the

revelation that vampire Tania is their daughter is downplayed, omitting the story of exactly how the couple is blackmailed to play along with the kidnapping of Marianne. The sure hand of a Jimmy Sangster might have crafted a script minus these flaws and thus created a more satisfying production.

Terence Fisher's 1960 *Curse of the Werewolf*, and not *The Phantom of the Opera*, was the Hammer director's first misfire, a production that wanted so desperately to deliver so much more than it did. By far the longest film on this collection, *Curse of the Werewolf* suffers from too much plot, tepid pacing and a lack of keystone sequences that became the focus of most Hammer productions. While *Curse of the Werewolf* offers some creative high points via performance, direction and cinematography, it suf-

fers the bane of the worst Hammer offerings… the film seems overlong and boring.

The film's first act is most intriguing, featuring the wonderful Richard Wordsworth as the beggar who crashes the high society wedding party of the perverse Marques (Anthony Dawson in a wonderful supporting performance) and finds himself locked in jail, eternally. When the buxom jailer's daughter (Yvonne Romain) refuses to sexually satisfy the festering Marques, she is thrown in the jail and savagely raped by the beggar, now more beast than human. Heaving and sweaty, the jailer's daughter is returned to the Marques, but instead of sexually submitting to him, she stabs the old bastard to death. However, she is now pregnant and has the misfortune to give birth on Christmas day, thus giving birth to a werewolf. The mother dies at childbirth but the kindly Don Alfredo (Clifford Evans) and his wife adopt the young child who is christened Leon (growing up to be the husky Oliver Reed). The period detail and perversity of performance and action maintain keen interest. Unfortunately, the middle third of the film crawls at a snail's pace, featuring a few sheep whose throats have been ripped out and a few sequences with the haunted young Leon sporting fangs after somnambulistic wanderings. Even when the now fully grown Leon leaves home to make his way in the world, the action of bonding with a buddy and finding work is simply the type of non-action for which Hammer deserves criticism. By the time Leon transforms into wolf, the film has simply lost viewer attention, and it does not help that most of the initial werewolf murders only show victims' reactions or outline the wolf in shadow. Terence Fisher is a master at maintaining a horrific mood and the murders are well staged. The sets are also excellent in period detail.

When the werewolf itself is shown (absolutely the best makeup execution ever by Roy Ashton and one of the best classic monsters in horror history), the film becomes a Hammer classic for about 20 minutes (and 20 classic minutes do not a classic film make). Oliver Reed's physique immeasurably helps the werewolf performance, with his hulking presence towering over the others in the cast. The use of gray fur and a partially open shirt produce a savage monster. The werewolf makeup comes to life in the carefully executed face, with lots of salvia flowing from the mouth, making the werewolf appear more animal than human. Reed (and his double?) breathes life into the makeup and brings his werewolf to startling life. Unfortunately the wolf is not seen very often in close-up, and it most deservedly should be. However,

Arthur Grant's cinematography following the werewolf across Spanish rooftops ultimately making his way to the church bell tower is spectacular and gives the film a sense of depth. Even Clifford Evans' dramatic rifle shot rips into the beast's body and kicks Reed on his ass within seconds. It's a powerful sequence and seldom has a rifle shot been filmed this violently on the screen. If the movie contained more active werewolf action, *Curse of the Werewolf* might have been a classic. However, in its current overlong and dead-in-the-middle plot structure, *Curse of the Werewolf* is a generally dull werewolf movie that sports one of the best lycanthropic makeups ever executed. That's worth something, isn't it?

Hammer's 1962 production of *Phantom of the Opera*, the first commercial fiasco directed by Terence Fisher, was the proof that not everything that Hammer touched turned to gold. And insiders say that because of the financial nose-dive at the box-office, Terence Fisher was not given new projects by Hammer, who thought that their maestro lost his golden touch. To be honest, *Phantom of the Opera* is an adequate chiller and sports a superb cast. Herbert Lom, before his success with the *Pink Panther* movies, plays the phantom and does a superb job. The scenes in his underground lair, in sequences where he plays dramatic, spooky music on the organ, are classic. Supporting characters include Patrick Troughton and Michael Ripper. Edward de Sousa, soon to star in *Kiss of the Vampire*, plays the male lead. The rather bland Heather Sears plays the heroine, the love object of the obsessed phantom. Michael Gough plays a sinister villain to utter perfection and the always-reliable Thorley Walters is much more subdued than he usually is.

The film's climax, where Heather Sears, alone on stage, is ready to be crushed by the dangling chandelier, is very tense and well photographed. For simple dramatic effect, Herbert Lom tears off his mask revealing his scarred face, and he darts down upon the stage majestically just in time to push Sears out of harm's way before

he is crushed by the shattering glass and metal. A nice climax to an obviously artier Hammer production, a movie that attempted to push the romance and angst forward and subdue the horror quotient. The sets are marvelous and the cinematography by Arthur Grant is first rate. But this *Masterpiece Theater* approach to Hammer horror was a compromise no one enjoyed. The fans of *Brides of Dracula* and the other Gothics found *Phantom of the Opera* too talky, too slow and too tame to interest them. And the production, hampered (and actually transcending) by a low budget, did not have the spectacle to rope in the more mainstream movie fan. So while Hammer was obviously trying to move subtly from exploitation to literary drama, the experiment was less than successful and *Phantom of the Opera* proves to be a Hammer production that fails because it tries to be too many things to too many people. Still, the production has moments of tension and horror and Herbert Lom becomes a quite sympathetic Professor Petrie who loses his life's work to a money-grubbing entrepreneur and eventually sacrifices everything for the love of the beautiful singer Christine (Sears).

Freddie Francis, one of cinema's most creative cinematographers, was unfortunately not one of its best directors; however, *Paranoiac*, a seldom-seen Hammer psychological thriller, is one of Francis' best efforts and is one Hammer treasure waiting to be rediscovered. Its widescreen black-and-white presentation is flawless, showcasing a pristine print featuring superb cinematography by Arthur Grant (with much influence by Francis himself). The dynamic musical score by Elisabeth Lutyens (notice how the Universal Hammers did not feature many musical scores by James Bernard) certainly helps to punctuate the excellent script by Jimmy Sangster (certainly one of his best).

*Paranoiac* was released in 1963 and follows in the creative wake of Alfred Hitchcock's *Psycho*, released three years earlier in 1960. The involved plot involves family grief and madness over the deaths of parents and the suicide (or was it?) of younger son Tony. The family is spiritually

ripped apart when sister Eleanor (Janette Scott) begins to see visions of the now adult Tony and questions her own sanity.

Equally traumatized brother Simon (Oliver Reed fresh from his success in *Curse of the Werewolf* and *Night Creatures* for Hammer) buries himself in guilt over the death of his brother Tony. Oliver Reed's screen persona was literally created by this movie. He plays the deeply romantic and troubled young man (who beds the French housekeeper, the sensual Liliane Brousse) who has a cigarette or drink in hand in virtually every scene (and in most he holds both). Reed's persona of the hard-boozing, self-centered hedonist was created right here. And his performance smolders as he descends into effective over-the-top insanity. In his most delicious sequence, for a few glorious seconds, Reed descends the family stairs cackling, eyes rolling in what otherwise might be considered a ridiculous interpretation of insanity. But for these wondrous seconds the descent (quite literally) into madness works.

Reed does not believe that his French lover is planning to stick around after she dared to leave him only a night before, but he makes love to her by the family duck pond. In a very interesting point-of-view shot, we see Simon bend Francoise's head back into the water. And then we see Francoise's point of view as the camera, underwater, looks up at the crazed Simon holding her head underwater until she drowns. At the appropriate moment all the ducks, in unison, make a sound approximating Bernard Herrmann's *Psycho* music score, creating a wink juxtaposed to one of the more creative murders in screen history.

But the sequences of true horror are reserved for the mysteries to be revealed in the deteriorating organ cottage that sits outside the main estate house. Inside Simon, in a daze, plays his organ creating frantic music that mirrors his emotional state. When returning brother Tony (or an imposter?) and Eleanor interrupt Simon, they encounter the terrifying form of a choir-robbed figure sporting a smiling stone mask, and the figure is holding a metal hook to be used as a weapon. Before long a decaying corpse is discovered behind the organ pipes that reveals the ultimate secret of the family that holds more than one skeleton is its closet.

The plot keeps the audience guessing, the surprises abound, the performances teeter on the edge and innocent and not-so-innocent people deceive the unwary. In a sense the film is little more than an exercise in technique and style, but with such well-drawn characterizations and performances (especially Oliver Reed and Janette Scott), *Paranoiac* becomes a movie that grows more intense and interesting as time goes on.

Unfortunately, lightning does not always strike twice, as now writer/producer Jimmy Sangster and director Freddie Francis teamed up for *Nightmare*, a film similar in style to *Paranoiac* but a film that contains little of its predecessor's charms. *Nightmare* opens with its defining sequence, a vivid black and white widescreen (Francis always likes to work in widescreen, and black and white became a requirement in the wake of Hitchcock's *Psycho*) nightmare featuring lovely Jennie Linden (as Janet) imagining herself, nightgown garbed, roaming the dank corridors of a mental institution, hearing the voice of her mother as Janet tries to find the padded cell where she has been confined. Once Janet enters the cell and the door slams behind her, the obviously insane mother states, "Now they got us both, as it should be!" This opening sequence, overtop the credits, is mesmerizing and sets the tone for the psychological drama to follow. Janet, a student at a private girls' school, wakes up screaming in the middle of the night, and before long, she is asked to remove herself from the school in order to seek out treatment. A sympathetic teacher drives her to her foreboding estate home where the nightmares continue. In the middle of the night a strange female figure, with a large facial scar, silently stalks the young girl, who soon believes that she too, like her mother, is going insane. Janet follows the strange woman to a bedroom where the woman lies dead, a knife in her chest, as a fully decorated birthday cake glows alongside the bed. In sheer terror, Janet runs out of the room. When the housekeeper catches up with her, Janet is out of her mind laughing hysterically and is soon confined to bed and medicated by the family doctor. The next night the same nightmares again occur with the same woman found dead with a knife in her chest. This time Janet is sent over the edge. But when the scarred woman appears at Janet's birthday party, the distraught girl picks up the huge knife lying next to her cake and plunges the blade into the woman's chest. In the next sequence Janet is being lifted out of her home on a stretcher to be taken to the asylum. However, this same strange and unidentified woman is standing at the window glaring downward as Janet is being carted off. Inside people are cleaning up as the scarred woman lifts a lifelike plastic mask off her face to reveal Grace inside (the woman sent to take care of Janet as she mends). Janet's lawyer guardian Henry (David Knight) and his wife Grace (Moira Redmond) are in cahoots to drive the poor girl insane, and they have succeeded.

So far the movie has been excellent, very suspenseful and mysterious in a stark visual sense, and the poor, pathetic Janet has been the catalyst holding the audience's sympathy and concern. However, now with her committed and out of the picture, the second half of the film involves mysterious parties who pull the same pranks on Janet's tormentors. Thus, the film's second half repeats the gimmick of the first, but the victims are evil and unsympathetic, so while our hearts went out to the poor victimized student, we secretly wish that Henry and Grace die horrible deaths in the film's second half. What we have here is half a wonderful film, and while the film's second half is not bad, it lacks the originality and emotional involvement provided during the first half. Freddie Francis' direction and the stark composition of the film are pluses that elevate the film above the generic.

*Night Creatures*, an odd duck Hammer production, pretending to be a pirate movie (in the same vein as *Pirates of Blood River*) but without showing any pirate ships or actual pirates, tends to go for horror overtones by featuring a few scenes with Marsh Phantoms (actually human

beings wearing luminescent glow-in-the-dark skeleton outfits). The film, directed by Peter Graham Scott, does not even play like the typical Hammer production, although the presence of Peter Cushing, Oliver Reed, Yvonne Romain and Michael Ripper makes it look like one. Peter Cushing's conversion from bloodthirsty pirate to reformed minister is one of Cushing's splashier performances, his dual lifestyles continuously clashing. He is the leader of a band of smugglers who fight British oppression and unfair taxation, yet his hell and brimstone preaching makes him the moral universe of the small cove-side town. At the same time he attempts to protect his daughter Imogene (Romain) from learning his identity and helping her escape the curse of Captain Clegg and preventing the sins of the father from falling upon the young girl. Cushing's performance is another high energy one with complex moral ambiguities, making his lead character heroic but terribly flawed. Oliver Reed's romantic lead is perfect and his physical suffering for his love makes the youthful Reed dashing as he's never been before. Michael Ripper, for once, gets an actual character to develop, and his friendship with Clegg is richly etched, especially in the film's final seconds when he carries the corpse of his friend to his grave, tears welling up in his eyes.

The film's typical Hammer touch and also its flaw is the presence of Tor Johnson Brit clone Milton Reid as the Mutallo, the man who dared attack Clegg's wife and received the punishment of having his tongue cut out and being left for dead. Now, years later, he only lives for revenge, and his weapon of choice is a steel spear that he wields with expert skill. Somehow his presence seems to be monstrous in a film that focuses on human beings, and his character appears in the film for only two reasons—to provide the horror aspect and to create a way to kill off the sympathetic and now reformed Clegg in a dramatic conclusion.

The sequences of the Marsh Phantoms are wonderfully photographed, garish and blinding as their ectoplasmic forms radiate, frightening all those who face these specters on horseback. Of course the audience understands immediately that these

are smugglers wearing glowing costumes, but the manner in which they are photographed is always spooky and demands our attention. Unfortunately, the film opens with one of these sequences and it would seem, in such a talky production, that perhaps it might have been better to hold off, for pacing's sake, on such splashy sequences for insertion later on.

*Night Creatures* has been built up to be a better film than it actually is because of its scarcity on home video; however, the wonderful Eastmancolor print is deeply saturated and generally blemish free. However, the film is never better than a good programmer with a few excellent performances. While it is indeed a treat to see such a fine DVD release, the film tends to be talky in parts and lacks a few needed action sequences that would have created the swashbuckling thrill sorely missing from the production.

Finally, the Hammer Collection comes to a wonderful conclusion with the too often criticized *Evil of Frankenstein*, a movie that has always been far better than the treatment it receives from fans. *Evil of Frankenstein* is the only Baron Frankenstein movie not directed by Terence Fisher, but Freddie Francis does a fabulous job of keeping the series vital and interesting. Surprisingly, this Hammer production is not widescreen, Francis' preferred cinematic palette. Basically, the plot is up to snuff, and Peter Cushing's performance as the Baron is both brooding and romantic, the film beginning with a dramatic sequence where an obsessive priest trashes the Baron's laboratory and destroys his detached human heart, causing the Baron to fling himself at the priest and wrap both hands around the clergy's throat. Such sequences of intensity and passion help define the character of Baron Frankenstein, a man who does not tolerate fools or misguided morality easily. He is truly the isolated scientist who wants to simply be left alone to conduct his experiments. However, his frozen and now thawed experiment, the revived Frankenstein Monster, is the basis of all the controversy. Since Universal was releasing the film in the States, the copyrighted Universal monster makeup could be approximated, but Roy Ashton was never given the final go-ahead with his test makeups, so the final makeup used appears half-baked. Yes, we have the square-headed monster, portrayed by Kiwi Kingston, but it is rather silly looking and is definitely a case of monster overload. However, how the monster is used and Kingston's acting is rather interesting and becomes a performance that overcomes bland makeup execution. And besides, the focus is always on Peter Cushing who commands every sequence and second he is onscreen. Katy Wild as a beautiful peasant deaf-mute is also an awkward choice. Her presence is a blatant excuse to evoke sympathy, establishing a beauty-and-the-beast relationship. Her performance is too self-conscious and she sometimes makes the audience uncomfortable.

Cushing's performance differs from some of the other performances in Terence Fisher's movies because he becomes at times the rogue hero, almost cast in the style of Errol Flynn, who is both anti-social and heroic. Professor Zoltan (Peter Woodthorpe) provides the villainy as the mesmerist who is needed to animate the monster. Instead of following the Baron's instructions merely to restore the monster to full consciousness, Zoltan uses the monster as his agent of vengeance, the hulking reborn forced to steal for the greedy con artist. Also the Burgomaster and the Chief of Police, figures of authority, become villainous when the Baron returns to his chateau and discovers all the treasures of his castle are now in the hands of these legal criminals. Baron Frankenstein, monster-maker, earns our sympathy and maintains it. The Baron, now in need of money, is cast as the victim, his total devotion to his work rendering him worthy of our respect. Thus the monster is misused, hypnotized by the professor and not the Baron, and the Baron becomes a noble character, the closest thing to a hero in the movie. And by the film's fiery climax, the Baron's self-sacrifice to save his friends makes him truly noble. *Evil of Frankenstein* is not the best Hammer production by far, but its fascinating sets (featuring Hammer's best laboratory, nicely photographed in color), fast pacing, wonderful Peter Cushing performance, inventive script, creative photography and direction makes for a wonderful addition to Hammer's Frankenstein series. And what is interesting is Hammer's take on mimicking the Universal Frankenstein. Unlike most of the other entries, *Evil of Frankenstein* features a true monster and large-scale laboratory that mimics the Universal flavor.

Once again extras are minimal on this boxed set, but the packaging and pressings of each movie are optimal (and observing original aspect ratios is another kudo). And to sell the set for basically $25 is a steal. For all Hammer horror fans, this might be the release of the year. The only downside is the overuse of compression to fit these movies onto only two discs, which causes tracking problems on some players.

www.ingramcontent.com/pod-product-compliance
Lightning Source LLC
Chambersburg PA
CBHW081728100526
44591CB00016B/2541